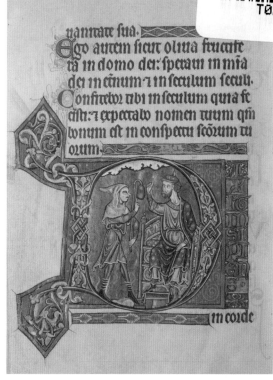

SIMPLES AND RARITIES SUITABLE AND HONOURABLE TO THE COLLEGE

First published in Great Britain in 2018 by Little, Brown

Copyright © Royal College of Physicians, 2018

The moral right of the author has been asserted.

Unless otherwise indicated, all images are from the RCP collections and photography is by Mike Fear.

Designed by Emil Dacanay and Sian Rance, D.R. ink

A CIP catalogue record for this book is available from the British Library.

ISBN 978-1-4087-0638-1

Printed in China

COVER: The Dorchester Library contains printed books and archival material from the thirteenth to the twenty-first century. This collection has benefited from the generosity of individual collectors, such as Matthew Baillie (1761–1823)
INSIDE COVER: Printer's marbled paper covering a seventeenth-century copy of *Cerebri anatome* (1680) (© Alastair Compston)
PAGE 1: Illumination from the Wilton *Psalterium*: King David arguing with a fool (Psalm 53), at folio 66 *verso*
OPPOSITE: Bookplate of College library

500

REFLECTIONS ON THE RCP 1518-2018

SIMPLES AND RARITIES SUITABLE AND HONOURABLE TO THE COLLEGE

Alastair Compston

Royal College of Physicians

Illustissimus · D · D ,
Henricus   Marchio ,

Durnovariæ ,

FOREWORD

The Royal College of Physicians was founded, by Royal Charter, in 1518 by King Henry VIII. Few professional organisations have been in continuous existence for so long, and over its five-hundred-year history the College has been at the centre of many aspects of medical life. Its principal purpose is to promote the highest standards of medical practice in order to improve health and healthcare, and its varied work in the field is held in high regard. Currently, the College has over thirty thousand members and fellows worldwide. Over the years it has also accumulated a distinguished library, extensive archives and a collection of portraits and other treasures, and has been housed in a number of notable buildings. As part of its quincentennial commemoration, a series of ten books has been commissioned. Each book features fifty reflections, thereby making a total of five hundred, intended to be a meditation on, and an exploration of, aspects of the College's work and its collections over its five-hundred-year history.

The College's Dorchester Library houses an outstanding collection, especially of medical books, and is one of the best in Britain. It contains manuscripts, incunabula, pamphlets and printed books, at least one hundred of which date from before the Great Fire of London, and accessions continue. Books are the lifeblood of any academic institution, and the historical library, together with the College's modern collection, express the continuous thread of scholarship in medicine and are central to the value and meaning of the College. Alastair Compston, as well as being a distinguished neurologist, is also a bibliophile. This volume on the topic of the medical book and the Dorchester Library is at once fascinating and beautiful, learned in content and lively in style. It describes not only the library and books, but also their significance and the how and the why of collecting. It is an original and brilliant addition to the five hundred years of College scholarship.

I must also offer grateful thanks to all who helped in the production of this book, and especially to Julie Beckwith, Head of the College Libraries. Thanks too are due to Linda Luxon, who has been intimately involved in the production of the series, and to the staff in the medical publishing department, and particularly to Karen Porter and the freelance designer, Sian Rance.

Simon Shorvon -

Simon Shorvon
Harveian Librarian 2012–16, Royal College of Physicians
Series Editor

OPPOSITE: Henry Pierrepont, Marquis of Dorchester (1606–80)

CONTENTS

Acknowledgements 8

THE MASTER PRINTER AND THE BOOK TRADE 10

THE LIBRARIES OF THE ROYAL COLLEGE OF PHYSICIANS 21

FIFTY ITEMS FROM THE LIBRARY OF THE ROYAL COLLEGE OF PHYSICIANS 32

THIRTEENTH CENTURY 34

Avicenna [Ibn Sīna] (980–1037). [Canon of medicine]. 35
[Anon]. [Psalterium]. 36

FIFTEENTH CENTURY 38

Raoul Le Fèvre (fifteenth century). [The recuyell of the histories of Troye]. 39
St Augustine of Hippo (354–430 AD). [De civitate Dei]. 41
Lucius Mestrius Plutarchus (45–120 AD). [Vitœ]. 42
[Guillaume Guerson] (fifteenth century). [Instruction de bien dancer]. 43

SIXTEENTH CENTURY 44

Joannes de Ketham (fifteenth century). [Fasciculus medicinœ]. 45
Marcus Tullius Cicero (106–43 BC). [Opera]. 47
Leonhard Fuchs (1501–66). [Herbal]. 48
Thomas Raynalde (sixteenth century). [The birth of mankind]. 49
Jean Fernel (1497–1558). [De naturali parte medicinœ]. 51
John Caius (1510–73). [The sweating sicknesse]. 52
Gabriele Falloppio (1523–62). [Opera]. 53

SEVENTEENTH CENTURY 54

Josephus Struthius (1510–68). [The art of the pulse]. 55
Thomas Vicary (1490–1561). [The English man's treasure]. 56
[Anon]. [London pharmacopoeia]. 57
William Harvey (1578–1657). [De motu cordis]. 59
[Anon]. [The plague]. 60
Thomas Browne (1605–82). Religio medici. 62
Daniel Whistler (1619–84). [The rickets]. 64
Thomas Willis (1621–75). Cerebri anatome. 65
Thomas Salusbury (c.1625–c.1665). Bibliotheca Marchionis Dorcestriœ. 66
Marcello Malpighi (1628–94). [Opera omnia]. 67
Francis Bernard (1627–98). [Catalogue]. 68
Samuel Garth (1661–1719). [The dispensary]. 70

EIGHTEENTH CENTURY 72

[Middleton Massey] (1678–1743). [Catalogue]. 73
William Heberden (1710–1801). [Medical transactions]. 74
Albrecht von Haller (1708–77). [Bibliotheca medicinœ practicœ]. 75
William Hunter (1718–83). [The anatomy of the human gravid uterus]. 76
George Edwards (1694–1773). [A natural history of uncommon birds]. 78
Michael Servetus (c.1511–53). [Christianismi restitutio]. 80
Edward Jenner (1749–1823). [Regulations and transactions]. 82
Matthew Baillie (1761–1823). [Morbid anatomy]. 84

NINETEENTH CENTURY 86

Robert Willan (1757–1812). [On cutaneous diseases]. 87
Charles Bell (1774–1842). [Idea of a new anatomy of the brain]. 89
Augustus d'Este (1794–1848). [The case of Augustus d'Este]. 90
William Macmichael (1784–1839). The gold-headed cane. 91
Samuel Johnson (1709–84). [Sermons]. 92
Richard Bright (1789–1858). [Reports of medical cases]. 93
Rudolf Virchow (1821–1902). [Cellular pathology]. 94
William Munk (1816–98). [Munk's Roll]. 95
Andreas Vesalius (1514–64). [Tabulœ anatomicœ sex]. 96

TWENTIETH CENTURY 98

Horace Mallinson Barlow (1884–1954). [Bookplates]. 99
Joseph Frank Payne (1840–1910). [Catalogue]. 100
Archibald Garrod (1857–1936). Inborn errors of metabolism. 102
Joseph Frank Payne (1840–1910). [History of the College Club]. 103
Henry Head (1861–1940). Destroyers and other verses. 105
[Eric Gill] (1882–1940). [New Testament]. 106
Robert Platt (1900–78) et al. [Smoking and health]. 107
Douglas Black (1913–2002). [Harveian oration]. 108

Bibliography 110

ACKNOWLEDGEMENTS

I am grateful to Julie Beckwith and the library staff, Katie Birkwood and Pamela Forde, for making available printed books and archival material, and for their helpful advice; Karen Porter for meticulous and accurate proofreading; Aquarius Book Restorers for the figures on page 16; the Old Library, Jesus College, Cambridge for the figure on page 19; Henry Oakeley who kindly wrote notes on two items of botanical interest and read the typescript, and for many spirited conversations about books; Simon Shorvon who commissioned this book and was a source of constant encouragement; Roger Gaskell who corrected many technical and bibliographic details but bears no responsibility for errors that remain; and Jan van Gijn who commented on the text and oversaw accuracy of the Latin transcriptions. And I am especially grateful to Sian Rance for her creativity, attention to detail and responsiveness to suggestions in managing to accommodate so much material within the space limitations and for the aesthetic design of this book.

ABOVE: Stamp placed by order of 25 June 1708 on the title page of books in the library; arms of Henry Pierrepont, Marquis of Dorchester on the cover of Nicolo Cabei's *Philosophica magnetica* (1629); Royal College of Physicians' arms stamped in gold on the front cover of Adrianus Spigelius' *De humani corporis fabrica* (1627)
OPPOSITE: Baron Munchausen raising the College of Physicians and its fellows at dinner in Warwick Lane on 30 September [1785] from Raspe's *The surprising adventures of Baron Munchausen* (1930), page 72 (© Alastair Compston) (see also page 70)

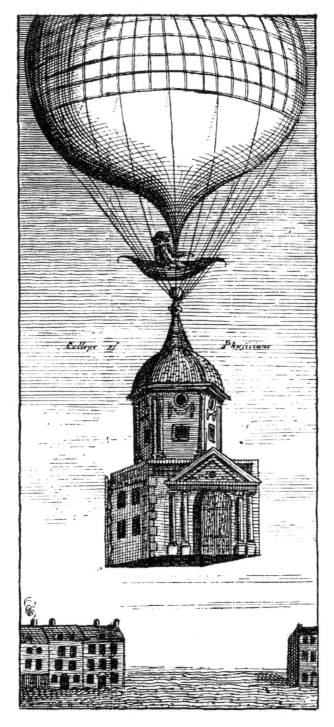

RAISING THE COLLEGE OF PHYSICIANS

THE MASTER PRINTER AND THE BOOK TRADE

Johañes Gutenberg m Strasburg. Erfinder der Edle Buchdruckerkunst Ano. Mccccl.

M.T.CICERONIS OPERA.

Ex Petri Victorii codicibus maxi-

The world changed when Johannes Gutenberg (c.1398–1468) first printed text using movable type. Print rapidly replaced the tradition of manuscript as the means through which the codex had been produced – and knowledge exchanged, archived and retrieved – over many centuries. Thereafter, despite the advent of wireless and television, print on paper remained the main medium for the communication of ideas until electronic transfer of information was introduced. Print reduced the cost of books. It promoted private ownership, expanded subject matter and stimulated the spread of literacy. Economic in its architecture, aesthetically pleasing and easy to handle, the well-constructed book is one of the great engineering feats of mankind.

Sometime around 1439, while living in Strasbourg, Gutenberg engaged in a new 'art and adventure'. He made multiple copies of individual characters in metal suitable for re-use. Gutenberg borrowed the idea of the screw press from Rhenish vintners. He introduced oil-based ink that adhered to lead alloy type and imprinted handmade rag paper. Back in Mainz by 1452, Gutenberg borrowed 1600 guilders from Johann Fust (1400–66) 'to finish the work'. Fust foreclosed on the loan and sued for return of his money and forfeiture of the printing tools and materials. Fust's son-in-law, Peter Schöffer (1425–1503), appeared as a witness. Despite these

tussles, the 42-line Bible appeared by 1456. Within a few years printing had spread to an estimated 250 towns in Europe.

The master printer's shop housed workers skilled in different trades. It was a hub of cultural and intellectual activity. The printer employed type founders, compositors, correctors, translators, copy editors, illustrators, indexers, artists and engravers. His shop was frequented by scholars, astronomers, physicians and priests; and it was a bookshop. Only papermaking and binding were trades plied elsewhere. It was not immediately obvious from examining early printed books who had written or produced the volume. The 'incipit' ('Hier begynneth') or first printed words of the text described what was to follow. The 'colophon' ('finishing stroke') contained details of the printer, place and date of production, and the patron. Additionally, the printer often identified himself

Economic in its architecture, aesthetically pleasing and easy to handle, the well-constructed book is one of the great engineering feats of mankind.

ABOVE: Jost Amman's woodcut illustration of the printer's workshop (© Ivy Close Images/ Alamy Stock Photo)
OPPOSITE TOP: Johannes Gutenberg (c.1398–1468) (© Heritage Image Partnership Ltd/Alamy Stock Photo)
OPPOSITE BELOW: House of Estienne: title page and printer's device from Cicero's *Opera* (1539)

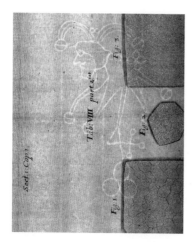

TOP: Watermark, the fool's cap from Willis'
Pharmaceuticae rationalis (1679): part 2, Tab VIII,
opposite D2r, page 17 (© Alastair Compston)
CENTRE: Arrangements on the forme, from
Gaskell (1972)
ABOVE: The printing press (© Deutsches
Museum, Munich, archive, BN24741)

with a woodcut device. Fust and Schöffer used a double shield hanging from a branch. William Caxton (1422–91) adopted a cryptic mark with 'W74C' as its central element. Aldus Manutius (1449–1515) used an anchor and dolphin. The device of Robert Estienne (1503–59) was an olive tree with a falling branch combined with the figure of a man. From the sixteenth century, the title page was used to name the book, its author and printer and the date of production. It might also promote the virtues of the volume and indicate where it could be purchased.

The punch-cutter carved and filed each letter or symbol in reverse on the end of a steel rod. This was then punched into a matrix fitted into a type-caster's mould into which a molten mixture of lead, tin and antimony was poured to produce individual characters, once more in reverse. The hardened metal character provided the movable type for impression on paper. Taking characters from his upper or lower case, the compositor placed letters and punctuation marks in a stick adjusted to the width of the page to be printed. He used whatever came to hand; chipped type, and both swash and non-swash capital italics. Lines were made up into pages arranged in a frame or chase. The individual pages were secured with wedges or quoins. Together, these created the 'forme' comprising all pages to be printed on one side of the same sheet. The assembled forme was then transferred to the press for printing. The outer forme was dabbed with 'ink-balls', placed on the tympan, and the impression created by the pressman pulling the bar to bring down the platen. Ideally, all copies of the outer forme required for a given edition were printed in one session. With the ink dry but the paper still damp, the sheets were printed on the reverse side with text making up the inner forme. During the press run mistakes might be corrected leading to slight variations between pages printed as part of the same edition. Larger corrections required a replacement, the cancel leaf.

7. Prouided alway, and be it enacted by Authority aforefaid, That it fhall be lawfull to any of the King's fubjects, not being Barber or Surgeon, to retain, haue and kǽp in his houfe, as his feruant, any perfon being a Barber or Surgeon, which fhall and may ufe and exercife thofe arts and faculties of Barbery or Surgery or either of them, in his Mafter's houfe or elfewhere by his Mafter's licence or commandment; Any thing in this Act aboue-written to the contrary notwithftanding.

Any perfon may keep a Barber or Surgeon as his Servant.

ℭ 2   34, 35 *H.* 8.

Letters and numbers; Roman, italic and old English type; signature and catchword from Goodall's *The Royal College of Physicians of London founded and established by law* (1684) at E2r, page 27 (© Alastair Compston)

Once printed and dry, the sheet was folded according to the format of the book: *folio* (folded once), *quarto* (twice), *octavo* (thrice), *duodecimo* (a complex structure with two additional leaves added to a four-leaf gathering). Therefore the printer had to impose the type pages in each forme so that, when printed and folded, the pages aligned on the *recto* and *verso* of each leaf and appeared in sequence. Signatures were added at the foot of the printed page, using the twenty-three letter Latin alphabet (A–Z, omitting I or J, U or V, and W; and then Aa–Zz, Aaa–Zzz, etc.) to aid the binder in ensuring that the order was correct. Catchwords served much the same purpose. Pagination provided another check on accuracy in the sequence of bound leaves but this was prone to error. The method for making paper left traces of lines where the pulp was suspended and spread across a frame before drying. Each sheet had a watermark, which identified its source, imposed as part of the manufacturing process. Dimensions of the book varied somewhat depending on the size of the original sheet: in England these were royal, crown, imperial and foolscap.

Illustrations were produced separately from the text. Manuscripts were rubricated and illuminated with hand-painted miniatures. With the advent of printing, spaces were left in the text for figures, decorated initials and borders to be finished by hand.

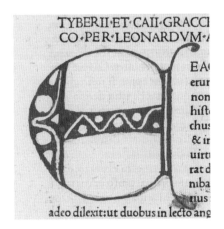

in the mid-nineteenth century. From these techniques evolved offset photolithography, the process used to print most modern books.

The practice of distributing unbound printed sheets to several booksellers led to variant title pages and non-uniform binding of sheets originating from the same edition. Books needed a cover to hold the gatherings in the desired order and to protect them from damage. Sewing through the folds with cords across the spine held the text-block together. This was covered with paper, but it was logical to place boards at the front and back secured to the loose

But it soon made sense for the image also to be printed from woodcuts. Pear, apple or boxwood was carved so that the lines remained in relief on the block. This was then locked into the forme and inked with the text for printing. Intaglio involved engraving lines on the surface of a metal plate (usually copper or, in the nineteenth century, steel) directly with a burin or by etching with acid, and pressing the dampened paper onto the plate so that it was forced into the inked grooves. Engravings from metal had to be printed on a rolling press, different from that used to print text and woodcuts. They could either be placed within spaces left in the letterpress or printed separately as full leaves and bound in as a secondary process. Engraving improved the level of detail needed for illustrating works on science and medicine. Invented late in the eighteenth century, lithography involved drawing with a greasy pencil onto limestone and watering the remaining surface so that ink was repelled, other than from the greased lines, during printing. Photography was introduced into book production

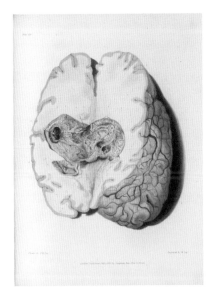

ABOVE: Chromolithograph from Bright's *Reports of medical cases* (1831), Volume II, Plate XXV, for which the original watercolour survives [MS974/95]
TOP LEFT: Initial letter added by hand (and smudged): from Plutarch's *Vitæ* (1478)
OPPOSITE: Heinricus Füllmauer (c.1505–46), Albertus Meyer (n.d.) [illustrators] and Veit Rudolph Speckle (n.d.) [block-cutter] from Fuchs' *Herbal* (1542)

TOP: Sewing of folded sheets, with hemp cords
ABOVE: Binders' tools used for finishing. (Both images © Aquarius Book Restorers, Essex)

ends of the cords, thus creating a hinged joint. Having forwarded the binding to this stage, it was finished by tooling, either with a blind stamp or gold leaf pressed into the leather with a heated tool. During forwarding, the edges of the leaves were usually cut by the binder to tidy up the uneven deckle edges and to remove the folds. In the eighteenth and nineteenth centuries books were sometimes sold with the edges unopened so that the reader had to use a paper knife to separate the pages as he or she read.

Book production changed with industrialisation. The manufacture of paper was mechanised and, with rags in short supply, wood was used. However, the need to treat the pulp with chemicals led to acidic paper that rapidly became brittle and survived poorly. Automated letter-founding culminated in the Linotype (line of type) and Monotype (each letter cast separately) systems that recycled type metal for recasting. Blocks of pre-set type were preserved by stereotyping for later reprinting of the same text. The steam-driven press was introduced for high volume work early in the nineteenth century. Perhaps more significant for the appearance of books and marketing strategies of publishers, binding cases of cloth over boards were made separately from the text-block, allowing the binding process to be automated and with all copies of an edition having a uniform appearance – often highly decorated. With the advent of electronic methods for typesetting and printing, these innovations were themselves adapted and replaced in the latter part of the twentieth century.

A degree of organisation occurred in England when the trades of text-writer, limner or illuminator, binder, bookseller and printer were regulated through a guild (dating in its early arrangements from 1403) that eventually became the Stationers' Company. This received its Royal Charter in 1557. Over time, the Company sought to monopolise what might legitimately be printed. Seditious and heretical material was suppressed. Booksellers produced listings, organised by subject or alphabet, to advertise their titles. Authors rarely benefited from sales or commissions but depended for their livelihoods on patronage. However, the Copyright Act for the Encouragement of Learning (1710) enfranchised the author. Increasingly, the codex became not only a repository of contemporary knowledge but also a treasure prized for its content and aesthetic qualities.

Medical content was present on Egyptian papyri. The subject flourished in Greece through the writings of Hippocrates (c. 460–370 BC) and Aristotle (384–322 BC); and in Rome with the work of Galen (c. 129–210 AD). Their

Riven oak-boards pasted to the text block with manuscript remainder from Cicero's *Opera* (1539)

The trades of text-writer, limner or illuminator, binder, bookseller and printer were regulated through a guild (dating from 1403).

influence reached well into the seventeenth century through the medium of print. Some novel works were written during the medieval period: treatises by Lanfranc of Milan (c. 1250–1306), Henri de Mondeville (1260–1320) and others. The introduction of printing did not immediately advance the dissemination of new scientific knowledge, readership remaining largely confined to scholars and physicians.

As the number of books increased, individual ownership became less feasible and readers turned to the library as a means of access. This repository of knowledge, organised and searchable, accommodated printed books, manuscripts and other archival material. At first, the items were stored in chests or cupboards. The furniture became more complex as its function as storage space and reading lectern evolved. Readers had their own carrels at which to work. Many books were chained. Eventually, books were piled horizontally or placed vertically, with the fore-edges exposed. Identification *in situ* required a short title to be written on the exposed leaves or, rarely, using a printed vertical half-title. Once books were shelved with their spines placed outermost, each was usually marked, externally or internally, with its shelf number.

As the number of books increased, individual ownership became less feasible and readers turned to the library as a means of access.

ABOVE: Chained library with fore-edges placed outermost (© Chetham's Library, Manchester)

BELOW: Lettering on the lower-edge of Fernel's *De naturali parte medicinæ* (1547)

With the founding of colleges dedicated to medicine, and hospitals and medical societies, the number of medical libraries increased. Because in many instances these collections

Shelving at Jesus College, Cambridge: the scrolls issuing from the beaks of the cockerels in the stained glass have texts from the Bible or the Church Fathers that give an indication of the manuscripts and books to be found by each window (© Jesus College, Cambridge)

With the founding of colleges dedicated to medicine, and hospitals and medical societies, the number of medical libraries increased.

began with donations, the subject matter was eclectic. The culture of endowment, more than acquisition policy, determined subsequent growth. Space was limited and books were traded or otherwise disposed of as new items became available. Some were discarded on doctrinal grounds. Others simply went astray. Indeed, the antiquarian book trade depended, then as now, on turnover to buy volumes and supply collectors. Libraries were not necessarily large: fewer than 200 books in the fifteenth century was significant but by the end of the seventeenth century an institution might claim to have 40,000 books. As the numbers increased, and location became more difficult, libraries produced catalogues to indicate their holdings. Gradually, collections that focused on science and medicine were formed; and several were donated, wholly or in part, to the Royal College of Physicians.

Stone House №5 Knightrider street, rebuilt after the Fire of London about 1670 on the site of the original College House (Linacre's House?) – enlarged from Dr. Macmichael's plate in the Gold headed Cane

see Vol. 1. page 238,

THE LIBRARIES OF THE ROYAL COLLEGE OF PHYSICIANS

When the College was founded in 1518, Thomas Linacre (c.1460–1524) made available his house in Knightrider Street, London. He designated one upper room as a library. This contained most of Linacre's medical books. Since books did not feature in his will (19 June 1524), it is presumed that the majority were already with the College. Other donations arrived before the Great Fire of London but space was at a premium and not all could be accommodated. William Gilbert (1544–1603) left an unspecified number in 1604; Matthew Holbosch (n.d.), a German who practised physic in England, bequeathed 680 volumes in 1629; and some of William Harvey's (1578–1657) books were added. Donation of manuscripts began with eleven belonging to John Selden (1584–1654). He had already helped the College to acquire Hebrew and Persian manuscripts; others came from William Rant (1604–53).

This was prompted by the letter from an anonymous benefactor proposing to build a library and repository 'for simples and rarities ... such a one as should be suitable and honourable to the College'.

At first the books were kept in a chest but, by 1632, they were in cases. On 4 July 1651, the President, Francis Prujean (1593–1666), asked the fellows whether they would agree to have a library built on or near the premises at Amen Corner, where the College had moved in 1614, if someone could be found to donate the funds. Presumably this was prompted by the letter from an anonymous benefactor proposing to build a library and repository 'for simples and rarities ... such a one as should be suitable and honourable to the College'. Located close to Stationers' Hall at Amen Corner and opened in February 1654, this was the first full classical building in England to contain a library. It was built to the design of John Webb (1611–72), pupil and successor of Inigo Jones (1573–1652). John Aubrey (1626–97) described it as 'a noble building of Roman architecture of Rustique work with Corinthian pilasters ... a great parlour of the Fellows to meet in belowe, and a library above'. Design drawings indicate a seven-bay rectangular building of two stories, the upper supported by an open arcade. Later sketches show this filled in to form the parlour described by Aubrey. Stalls and bays projected into the room, some but not all illuminated by natural light. It soon became apparent that the benefactor was William Harvey and, in 1654, the space was named the *Musæum Harveianum*.

Gualterus · Chartton · N

Harvey suggested that 'besides medical books we consider those to be especially useful and suitable for the Museum which deal with Geometry, or Geography, or Cosmography, or Astronomy, or Music, or Optics, or Natural History, or Physics or mechanics, or that treat of journeys to remote regions of the Earth'. He drew up rules for the use of his library. Statutes and regulations were approved in 1656 and a committee constituted together with statements on opening hours (Friday from 2 p.m. to 5 p.m., 4 p.m. in the winter; at Comitia meetings; or at the discretion of the librarian). The library and bookcases were to be locked. Books could be borrowed subject to a pledge of twice their value; or by fellows who had already donated five or more books.

Christopher Merrett (1614–95), also known as Merret, served as librarian from 1654 to 1666. He was recommended by Harvey and lived rent-free at Amen Corner. The College paid him £20 *per annum*. However, tragedy soon followed for, on Sunday 2 September 1666, fire broke out in the City of London and the College was engulfed. Sacrificing his own collection, Merrett attempted to retrieve items from the library as the flames licked around him. The archive, legal documents, charters and deeds were rescued but most of the books were lost. Based on the work of Miss Eleanor Boswell (n.d.) in 1929–30, it is estimated that only ninety-five items survived, of which fifty-eight remain in the College library. Every one of Linacre's books was burned (although the College has three others that belonged to him). One of Harvey's

annotated books was rescued. Despite the fact that there was now no library for him to curate, Merrett argued that he should retain for life the office of Harveian librarian and the £20 annual stipend, disregarding the statute that 'the term of life and of office [shall] be the same for the Custodian of this Museum unless for serious reasons it shall appear otherwise to the College'. Merrett kept hostage the books he had salvaged until the College took him to Chancery and won back its meagre remaining stock. Merrett ceased to attend Comitia and, in 1681, was removed from the fellowship to which he had been elected in 1651. But not all his work was in vain. Merrett is credited with having added molasses to wine in order to make it brisk, thus introducing the process by which champagne is made, a topic on which he lectured to the Royal Society in December 1662.

After the Great Fire, the College of Physicians moved to Warwick Lane. The building was designed by Robert Hooke (1635–1703). Eventually, the library was re-stocked through the donation of Henry Pierrepont (1606–80), created Marquis of Dorchester in 1645. An amateur physician, Dorchester collected books, read for much of the day, worked in his chemical laboratory and tended his botanic garden. He was made an honorary fellow of the College in 1658, perhaps at the suggestion of Harvey, adding £20 to his previous donation of £100. Dorchester indicated in 1679 that he might leave his books to the College but he hesitated since they could not be accommodated. The College was

ABOVE AND OPPOSITE TOP: Designs for the Musæum Harveianum by John Webb (1611–72)
(© The Provost and Fellows of Worcester College, Oxford)

therefore motivated to settle a boundary dispute with its neighbours in Warwick Lane. There was some urgency because the Marquis was unpredictable and, despite knowing that it was now rather short of books, the College feared that he might endow an Oxford College and fail to confirm the intended gift. There was panic when he nearly died of an accidental overdose of opiates. And, in December 1680, the Marquis did perish from gangrene superimposed on a sore leg caused by rubbing himself with salt. He was tended in his final illness by (Sir) Thomas Browne (1605–82) and his son Edward (1644–1708), who knew of and promoted the intended gift of books to the College while recognising that the price would be their adequate accommodation. In the event, the books did not feature in Dorchester's will but a deathbed assurance to Edward Browne secured the donation. This reflected the generosity of the main beneficiary of the estate, Dorchester's daughter Lady Grace Pierrepont (c.1635–1703). However, the new College building in Warwick Lane had no provision for a library and, in any event, its few surviving books were still in the possession of Christopher Merrett. A small room contained legal documents and the Annals. Therefore, in response to the Dorchester donation, the College commissioned Christopher Wren (1632–1723) to create a library in Hooke's building. There is some confusion as to where exactly this was placed and whether a new room was built. It seems that Wren suggested converting existing

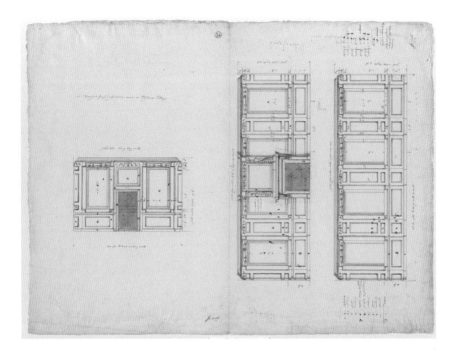

space (the kitchen with its chimney removed), designating two rooms and a gallery in the main building. The books started to arrive on 4 December 1686 and were placed on 900 feet of shelving designed for folios, quartos and octavos, respectively. Everything was in place by February 1687, a ledger having been purchased on 19 December 1686 in which a catalogue was to be written. The hope was expressed that Lady Grace Pierrepont would visit the College and admire the fruits of her benefaction.

Walter Charleton (1619–1707) had been proposed as the keeper of Dorchester's books on 9 April 1688 (Dorchester had been his patron) but he was not appointed until 6 December 1706, with a retainer of £20 *per annum*. Sadly,

Christopher Wren (1632–1723) (© National Portrait Gallery, London)

Charleton only received the first two instalments of £5 since, already aged eighty-seven, he died five months later. Charleton had been turned down for the fellowship on the basis that his writings offended the Church. When, despite this transgression, he did later become President, Charleton was something of an absentee, spending much of his time in the Channel Islands having fallen on hard times. A committee charged with looking after the library reported on 25 June 1708 and requested an under library keeper to catalogue the books; to maintain an inventory of acquisitions and disposal of duplicates (not to include any Dorchester books); to keep the place clean and tidy with no candles or tobacco-smoking; and to mark each title page with the College stamp.

In November 1710 this committee recommended 'that if hereafter it shall be thought convenient to join this place with that of the Bedell of the College, then the expence of the College hereby will be lessen'd, and by having a Lodging at the College he will be ready at hand on all occasions'. Thus, the office of Harveian librarian now lapsed. Nonetheless, having decided that the Bedell should take charge, Richard Tyson (c.1680–1750) – previously appointed curator of the library while also acting as Registrar, Treasurer and President – was appointed, and served from 1734 to 1750. Tyson was able to expand the library through a benefaction of £450 bequeathed to the College for the purchase of books by his uncle Richard Hale (1670–1728).

It seems likely that some books belonging to the College wandered to Sloane's home and found their way from there to Montague House, which became the British Museum.

The library continued to grow through donation, but not every collector was philanthropic. With an interest in botany (Sir) Hans Sloane (1660–1753) came to know the Chelsea Physic Garden, which was then managed by the Company of Apothecaries. He was President both of the Royal College of Physicians and the Royal Society and renowned for his collections of antiquities, coins, medals, crystals, gems, and botanical and zoological specimens. He is said to have had a library of 40,000 volumes, including 3700 manuscripts, with many presentation copies from the most celebrated physicians and scientists of the day. It seems likely that some books belonging to the College wandered to Sloane's home and found their way from there to Montague House, which became the British Museum. Richard Mead (1673–1754) accumulated 10,000 volumes, which were sold on his death for £5,518.18s.11d at a sale lasting several weeks from 18 November 1754. The manuscripts were sold to Anthony Askew (1722–72). Many books went to the Medical Society of London. Thomas Crow[e] (1671–1751) left £50 and his library of Greek and Latin books to the College of Physicians: 'such of my printed books as have no English in them and as they have not already in their library … or if mine be better copies, though they have them already'. Three months were allowed for (Abraham) Hall (d. 1751), Thomas Reeve (1700–80) and (Joseph) Letherland (1699–1764) to execute the will. They were required to catalogue the books but, as so often happened, this document never materialised or is now lost, although fourteen books containing Crowe's inscription can still be identified.

THE NEW COLLEGE OF PHYSICIANS, PALL MALL, EAST.
TO ROBERT BREE M.D THIS PLATE IS MOST RESPECTFULLY INSCRIBED.

Published April 23 1825 by Jones & C⁰ 3 Acton Place Kingsland Road London.

Although the emphasis remained on medicine, the College library was a haphazard collection, neither primarily a working library nor shaped to some specific acquisitions policy. Its standing was now eclipsed by collections of the Royal Society and the ascendency of the British Museum. New statutes in 1765 made the librarian responsible to Comitia and relaxed somewhat the rules on borrowing. A book could be had in exchange for the payment of £2 but with fines levied for late returns. Fellows were assigned responsibility for the library but no one was elected to the post named after Harvey. The most diligent of these was John Latham (1761–1843). Expenditure in the library was limited to around £20 *per annum* and any additional income derived from funds received by the College for the inspection of madhouses. By 1814, Latham, now President, became concerned about the library, managed by a series of Bedells, and appointed as custodian the Registrar, requiring him to be resident.

When the College moved to Pall Mall East in 1825, the library was set to benefit through having much larger and more prominent accommodation. However, during the move all

When the College moved to Pall Mall East in 1825, the library was set to benefit through having much larger and more prominent accommodation.

Over his forty-one-year tenure, Munk gave the library prominence as a resource of material on medical history.

the books were stored in the house of William Behnes (1795–1864), sculptor, in Gerrard Street, Soho. A significant number were stolen. Still with an erratic purchasing policy, the emphasis on medicine and its history gained momentum when, in 1823, Mathew Baillie (1761–1823) gave all his medical, chemical and anatomical books – fifty manuscripts and 900 printed volumes, mainly published during his lifetime but with a good number from the sixteenth century or earlier – to the College together with his anatomical preparations, the gold-headed cane and an endowment of £300. The new accommodation provided improved space for the books, arranged in ten sections by subject but with shelving by size. A committee met on 22 December 1818 reporting on deficiencies in the holdings of modern works on the main subjects of interest. It created a list that fellows might supply and suggested that books of which there were more than two copies be sold to fellows in order to raise funds for other purchases. This was considered sensitive and it was agreed that all such sales should be kept secret. The aim between 1825 and 1846 was therefore to create a modern medical library rather than nurturing an historical resource.

In 1857 the College revived the post of Harveian librarian, arguing that a doctor was needed to supervise a medical library. William Munk (1816–98) was chosen because of his interest in medical biography. He served until

1898. His great contribution was the *Roll of the Royal College of Physicians of London* (1861–75). Munk took 'little interest in the present degenerate race of physicians ... my memoranda are limited almost exclusively to physicians who joined the College in the old and regular way before 1825'. Over his forty-one-year tenure, Munk gave the library prominence as a resource of material on medical history. He defined a style and tradition of scholarship that, with some exceptions, has continued to epitomise the role of the Harveian librarian.

An interest in medical history was maintained by Munk's successor, Joseph Frank Payne (1840–1910), who served from 1899 to 1910. Payne wrote on medical history and was a bibliophile and collector. (Sir) Norman Moore (1847–1922) was Harveian librarian from 1910 to 1918 when he became President. Moore wrote a two-volume history of St Bartholomew's Hospital (1918). He persuaded the widow of Thomas Fitz-Patrick (1832–1900) to endow a lecture in medical history and he spoke on 'The history of the study of medicine in the British Isles' in 1908. As Harveian librarian from 1918 to 1944, Thomas Chaplin (1864–1944) collated and added to the collection of prints depicting medical and scientific people. His Fitz-Patrick lectures were on 'Medicine in the reign of George III' (1917–18). The post of Harveian librarian lapsed briefly after Chaplin's death. Archibald Gilpin (1906–1959) was a collector of books, furniture and clocks which eventually sold for £17,500. He was instrumental in reviving *Munk's Roll* confining the entries to fellows of the College, but illness forced him to resign after one year in post (1948–49).

As Harveian librarian from 1949 to 1962, (Sir) Charles Dodds (1899–1973) again orientated the College towards biography and medical history, sensibly leaving contemporary medical literature to other institutions. He employed the first professional librarian, Leonard Payne (1911–2000) as assistant. Payne was responsible for the transfer of 50,000 books, manuscripts and archives from Pall Mall East to the new building in Regent's Park. During his tenure, the practice of regular exhibitions selected from the College's holdings was instituted. Payne argued successfully for the appointment of a trained archivist to join the team working in the library. He was succeeded (under various titles of appointment) by Denis Cole, Geoffrey Davenport, Julie Beckwith, Sarah Griffin, Katie Flanagan and Katie Birkwood.

Charles Newman (1900–89) had a long and dedicated association with the College, including seventeen years as Harveian librarian (1962–79) during which, with Leonard Payne, he wrote systematically on its history in the College journal. He had found the College 'inert' when he became a member (1928) and fellow (1932), and was an advocate of appointing younger people to the fellowship. With others, he chose Denys Lasdun (1914–2001)

to design the building in Regent's Park. His Fitz-Patrick lectures (1954–5) were published as the *Evolution of medical education in the nineteenth century* (1957). Newman introduced recordings of oral history; and he would rarely forgo the opportunity of standing to address the fellows and their guests on books and his other interests in medieval architecture, painting, instrumental music and red wine during dinners at the College.

On assuming the post of Harveian librarian (1979–89), (Sir) Gordon Wolstenholme (1913–2004) persuaded the Treasurer to assign responsibility for portraits and the museum to the library, and he began a programme of conservation. Wolstenholme organised two publications on the portraits in the College (1964 and 1977). He initiated historical lectures that brought to attention holdings in the library, maintained the oral history programme and livened up the entries in *Munk's Roll*. (Sir) Christopher Booth (1924–2012) was a veteran user of the College library who wove historical threads into his many clinical and scientific lectures and papers. As Harveian librarian from 1989 to 1997, he introduced electronic methods and online searching, and organised the archives so that books, manuscripts and museum items could be located and used by researchers. Booth initiated interactions between the College and the Wellcome Trust Centre for the History of Medicine. He wanted to change the 'quill pen' culture of the

Payne was responsible for the transfer of 50,000 books, manuscripts and archives from Pall Mall East to the new building in Regent's Park.

ABOVE AND OPPOSITE: Eighteenth- and nineteenth-century ownership bookplates and shelf-marks: signatures of Sir Lancelot Browne (1545–1605) and Matthew Baillie (1761–1823) placed in their books

library into a modern technologically aware centre; and he emphasised the work and contribution of the library staff.

A lifelong interest in music, and contacts with the professional communities active in the arts, gave Ian McDonald (1933–2006) an unusually broad aesthetic perspective and, although not a bibliophile or collector, culture was the thread that ran through his tenure as Harveian librarian (1997–2004) in which he was conspicuous for wise counsel and loyal support of the College staff. The four living Harveian librarians (and their tenures of office) are Leon Fine (2004–07); Andrew Hilson (2008–12); Simon Shorvon (2012–16); and Simon Bowman (from 2016).

Prominent donors of books in the twentieth century included David Lloyd Roberts (1835–1920) who, in 1921, gave 1800 volumes including fifty-three incunabula, this being the largest such donation since the Marquis of Dorchester in the seventeenth century. Roberts' collection of Thomas Browne's works went to the John Rylands Library in Manchester; and his glass, watercolours and other pictures to colleges of the University of Wales. Other significant donors were Roy Dobbin (1873–1939), who collected manuscripts in Egypt and gave thirty-one (twenty-two Arabic and nine Persian) to the College; and Cyril Lloyd Elgood (1892–1970), who collected in Persia and donated one Arabic and nine Persian manuscripts. In 1951, the College's collection of manuscripts was catalogued by Arthur Tritton (1881–1973) for the *Journal of the Royal Asiatic Society*.

> *[manuscript annotation in medieval hand]*

fle hym Alas and yf y fle hym than hit femeth me y
fholdɔ refifte the wylle of the goddes whiche perauen
ture will repfe hym agayn Andɔ that foldɔ be worfe
forɔ than y foldɔ not only be callydɔ an homycidɔ andɔ
manflear but a vnnaturel murderer. not of a geant
norɔ of a ftrange man of a nother landɔ but of a right
litil childɔ yffuedɔ of my propre vaynes bones andɔ
fleffh. that after the prenoftication of the goddes is p
electe andɔ choffen to be the grettest lordɔ of grece andɔ
fouerani of all the kynges in his tyme.

Aturne thus felyng hym in grete forow a trow
ble andɔ alwey wores a wores as a fore is faydɔ

Annotation in text, Sir Nicholas Saunder (dated 1562) from Caxton's *The recuyell of the histories of Troye* (1473)

Over a period of 500 years, the library of the Royal College of Physicians has expanded from the contents of a chest in the upper floor of Linacre's house in Knightrider Street to the splendour of the Lasdun building in St Andrews Place containing printed books from 1473 to the present day, and a valuable archive of material in manuscript and other formats. Its history is part strategic and part the result of collectors' whimsicality, together resulting in a rich and important collection. The library has kept pace with changes in the trades of master printer, book publisher and illustrator. With occasional lapses, it has been curated by a series of physicians who knew and respected the history of medicine. It is not a comprehensive modern medical library and the occasional attempts to make it such have always been reversed by wiser and more enlightened leadership.

The library of the Royal College of Physicians has expanded from the contents of a chest to the splendour of the Lasdun building.

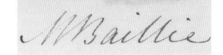

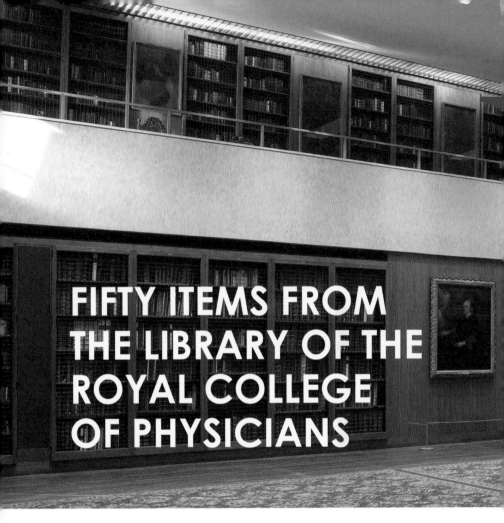

FIFTY ITEMS FROM THE LIBRARY OF THE ROYAL COLLEGE OF PHYSICIANS

The selection of fifty items that follows is representative of the collection in that it covers the thirteenth to the twentieth centuries; includes printed books and material in manuscript; describes some important books in the development of medical science but is not confined to material dealing with science and medicine; depicts the techniques of printing, illustration and binding; demonstrates the business of collecting and provenance; and records activities of the College in publishing and recording its own history. It is astonishing how often copies of important items, identified during reading and research, were to be found in the library. Another author would have had no difficulty in choosing an entirely different and equally representative selection of books and archival material. The descriptions may appear idiosyncratic to the professional bibliographer. Where the book has a title, this is given. For items that have an incipit or extended title page, this is reproduced but preceded by a working title in Latin or English depending on common usage. The place and date of publication are printed or taken from the colophon. The primary description

of English titles is in Roman type, contained within [brackets] where abbreviated, and those in other languages in *italics*; all other reference to the fifty items, in the text and captions, is in *italics* irrespective of language. The number of leaves and the pagination are given but not the signatures; and printers' errors are not listed. Measurements relate to the binding not the leaves. Any distinguishing features for the particular copy are described, together with the identifying number needed for location of that item in the College library. Almost without exception, each codex has the bookplate of the Royal College of Physicians stuck onto the front paste-down; and, as decreed in 1708, the title pages are stamped with the College coat of arms. Each has pasted in a small slip indicating the location, and many have earlier shelf-marks in ink or pencil. These recurring details are not mentioned in the descriptions that follow. In documenting the provenance, 'inscription' indicates ownership or entries unrelated to the content of the book, whereas 'annotation' denotes markings or commentaries that do relate to the text.

mea: 7 salus mea quem timebo.
Dominus protector uite mee: a quo
trepidabo.
Dum appropiant sup me nocen
tes: ut edant carnes meas.
Qui tribulant me inimici mei:

THIRTEENTH CENTURY

AVICENNA
[Ibn Sīna] (980–1037).
[Canon of medicine].

Al-qanun fi 'ilm al-tibb [Book 1 only].

Baghdad, Ali ibn Hasan ibn Musa'id. 611AH (1214).

Manuscript in Arabic. Folio, 184 leaves (paper), foliated as 184 in a later hand [folio 1 from another manuscript consists of: (1) anonymous notes on the humours of the body; (2) notes by Hibat allah ibn Sa'id on Avicenna. The leaves are bound in some disarray with discontinuities at folios 18, 160, 161 and 180 and with the colophon misplaced; some later leaves may be lacking]. 340 x 255 mm; text in 21 lines within 250 x 190 mm borders. Later blind-tooled calf and folding flap, rebacked and with extensive repairs to the boards and paper. [Triton 12].

Annotated: extensively in Latin and occasional Arabic, unattributed.

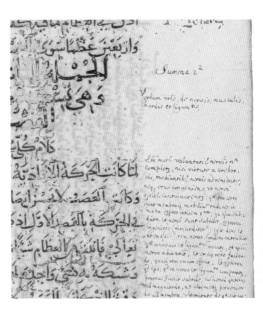

Avicenna was a physician, probably at one time to Abu Taleb Rostam (997–1029) the emir of Rey in Iran. The *Canon of medicine* is in five books: (1) on the generalities of anatomy and physiology; (2 and 5) on simple and compound drugs; and (3 and 4) on disease, arranged topographically. Largely theoretical rather than based on medical practice, the text is faithful to the teachings of Galen and Aristotle. Avicenna adopted the medieval cell doctrine of the brain, adding inner sense to the properties of the middle ventricle, responsible for imagination and thinking. He developed a concept of blood passing through the lungs from the right to the left side of the heart rather than across a septum between the ventricles. Dated 1214, this fragment of the *Canon of medicine* is the oldest item in the College library. It came from the estate of John Selden in 1654. The College also owns a thirteenth- or fourteenth-century Latin translation of Avicenna in manuscript written in Italy on thick parchment with red and blue initials (*Liber canonis primus … de medicina edidit translatus a magistro Girardo*, etc.). This was sold by T[homas] Thorpe in 1836 for £1.1s. 0d; and reappeared in the Phillips sale (MS 8786) on 27 April 1903 when it was bought by the College. It had been rebound by George Stoakley of Cambridge in 1889 for £1.10s. 0d (the firm remains in business). These two manuscripts are fully described in Peter Pormann's *The mirror of health* (2013), catalogue of an exhibition at the College, as items 5 and 8, pp. 21–5.

OPPOSITE: Illumination from the Wilton *Psalterium:* the Holy Spirit descending (Psalm 27), at folio 33 *recto*

[ANON]. *[Psalterium]*.

The Wilton psalter.

Salisbury. c.1250.

Manuscript in Latin. Folio, 229 leaves, foliated as v (plus iiia) 221 vi–vii [ii and iv are from Justinian *Institutiones*, Book I, sections xxi–xxiv, written in the thirteenth or fourteenth century; iii / iiia contain the beginning of a life of St Denis '(N)obilitatem quidem et preclarum in diuiciis beatissimi Dionysii' ..., written in the thirteenth or fourteenth century; v, originally blank, contains an account in 36 and 12 lines of the *Pater noster* in French written in a contemporary English hand of the fourteenth century], capitals illuminated mainly in red, blue and gold, and in various sizes (up to 12 lines), breaks between verses decorated, and with pen-work flourishes. 290 x 200 mm (the written space, 200 x 120 mm in 18 lines between double-ruled horizontal boundaries). Original parchment covers preserved within twentieth-century quarter morocco with blind and gilt-tooling, oak boards and clasps [Douglas Cockerell and Son 1950]. [MS409].

Inscribed: (1) This was my great grandmothers fathers booke and therefore for the antiquityes sake I keepe it. Nick Saunder; (2) R[alph] Lepton (twice); (3) Alresford, in a different hand, unattributed.

Annotated: (1) William Saunder, in Latin, an abnegation of the name Papist; (2) extensively by Ralph Lepton, rector of Alresford and Kings Worthy to Elizabeth Langrege, nun of Romsey, 1523, in Latin (at folio 144/5); (3) unattributed, in a different hand.

Monasteries made copies of texts by Christian authors for their own use, although scriptoria were also active outside these places. The scribe wrote in Latin, usually with Gothic script, using a quill pen obtained from swan, goose or turkey feathers. He held a knife for repeated sharpening and scraping errors off the page of the emerging leaf. His work was passed to the rubricator, who used red, blue and gold for enlarged initials, borders and headings; and then to the illustrator, who produced the miniatures. Patrons started to covet luxuriously illuminated devotional works such as psalters so that professional scribes and craftsmen supplemented activities

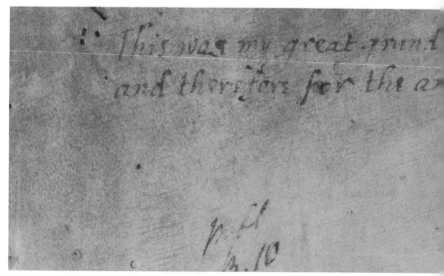

Provenance statement of Sir Nicholas Saunder, the younger (1563–1649)

previously confined to monks and nuns. This psalter is a richly ornamented manuscript written on vellum for use at Wilton Abbey in Wiltshire. Two half-page illuminations survive: the initial D at folio 33 describing *Dominus illuminato mea* (Psalm 27) depicts the Holy Spirit descending; and folio 66 shows King David arguing with a fool in the initial D of *Dixit insipiens in corde suo* (Psalm 53). Smaller miniatures appear elsewhere: an eagle taking a lamb in the initial C of *Cum invocarem* (Psalm 4) at folio 8; and a goat playing a viol in the D of *Deficit insalutare tuum anima* at folios 156 and 157. The Wilton *Psalterium* came from the Marquis of Dorchester's bequest and has the inscription of (Sir) Nicholas Saunder of Ewell who plundered John Dee's books, some of which did become part of Dorchester's library. It is not clear whether this copy once belonged to Dee since, unlike the known items, it does not have any relevant markings.

Patrons started to covet luxuriously illuminated devotional works such as psalters.

Quarter morocco with oak boards and clasps, binding by Douglas Cockerell and Son from 1950

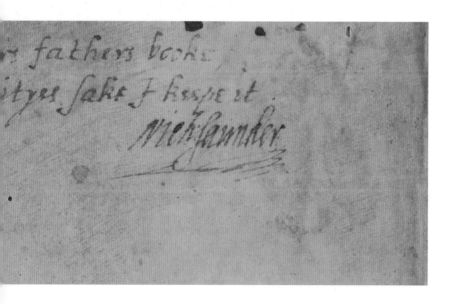

Cy finiſſent les regleſ de dācer toutes dāces
auecqs celles regles ſont notees pour Jouer
a tous Inſtrumens nouuellement iprimees
aparis aumont ſaīct hylaire par Michiel
tholouze alenſeigne de la corne du cer

:1488:

FIFTEENTH CENTURY

RAOUL LE FÈVRE (fifteenth century).
[The recuyell of the histories of Troye].

[Incipit (lacking from this copy)]: Here begynneth the volume intituled and named the recuyell of the historyes of Troye, composed and drawen out of dyuerce bookes of latyn in to frensshe by the ryght venerable persone and worshipfull man. Raoul le ffeure. preest and chapelayn vnto the ryght noble gloryous and myghty prynce in his tyme Phelip duc of Bourgoyne of Braban.

Bruges, William Caxton. 1473.

Folio, 352 leaves [lacks leaves 1 (blank), 2 and most of 8], foliated intermittently as 3, then on every fiftieth leaf to 300, and ending at 352, in a later hand, initials supplied in red and blue manuscript. 285 x 200 mm. Twentieth-century morocco with blind-tooling. [21999].

Inscribed: (1) Wm Saunder is owner of this boke; and with further note in his hand; (2) Margery Wellessbourne (several); (3) unattributed in two additional hands, on original vellum end-leaf.

Annotations: various, unattributed, in English and Latin.

William Caxton worked as cloth merchant and governor of the English merchants at Bruges. In 1469 he translated into English the compilation from Latin sources of *The recuyell of the histories of Troye* by Raoul le Fèvre (n.d.), chaplain to Philip, Duke of Burgundy (1396–1467). At the time, Caxton was employed as secretary to Margaret of York (1446–1503), sister of Edward IV (1442–83) and Duchess of Burgundy. One copy of the *Recuyell* has an inserted leaf depicting Caxton presenting the book to Margaret. This is the first book to be printed in English. Caxton started work on 1 March 1468 and completed the translation in Cologne on 19 September 1471. He tells us:

I have practised and lerned at my great charge and dispense to ordeyne this said book in prynte after the maner and form as ye may see here, and is not wreton with penne and ynke, as other books ben, to thende that every man may have them attones, for all the books of this storye named the Recule of the Historyes of Troyes, thus enprynted as ye here see, were begonne in oon day and also fynysshid in oon day….

ABOVE: Decorated initial from Le Fevre's *The recuyell of the histories of Troye* (1473)
OPPOSITE: Colophon from Guerson's *Instruction de bien dancer* (c. 1490) with incorrect date added in manuscript

Caxton shaped the English language with a change from phonetic to standardised spelling.

He may have been assisted by Colard Mansion (c.1440–84). In 1476, Caxton took his type to London and established a printing business at a shop in the Almonry, at the sign of the Red Pale near Westminster Abbey, producing his first book in 1477 [*Dictes or sayengis of the philosophres* by Earl Rivers (1442–83), Edward IV's brother-in-law]. Caxton introduced the ampersand (&) and other characters including ligatures and diphthongs (such as æ and œ). He printed ninety books, of which seventy-four were in English. Caxton shaped the English language with a change from phonetic to standardised spelling. But his books had many typographical errors often involving letters that are similar in appearance: 'p's and 'q's; 'b's and 'd's; and 'u's and 'n's. This copy of *The recuyell of the histories of Troye*, one of eighteen thought to have survived, was among items bequeathed to the College by the Marquis of Dorchester.

ABOVE: William Caxton (1422–91) (© National Portrait Gallery, London)
OPPOSITE: Decorated border, and colophon from St Augustine *De civitate Dei* (1473)

ST AUGUSTINE OF HIPPO (354–430 AD).
[De civitate Dei] (with the commentaries of Thomas Waleys and Nicolas Trivet).

[Incipit] Sententia beati augustini episcopi ex libro retractacionu[m] ip[s]ius de libris de ciuitate dei with the commentaries of Thomas Waleys and Nicholas Trivet. [Sacre pagine [pro] fesso[rum] … Thome valois & nicolai triueth in libros b[ea]ti augustini de ciuitate dei Co[m] me[n]taria].

[Colophon] Igitur aurelii Augustini … pcelsa in urbe mogutina: p[er] Petru schoiffer de gernsheim. Anno domini M.cccc.lxxiii. die.v. mensis septembris … Tenere aut ac gubernate xpiamsmi monarchias impatore seressimo Frederico tercio Cesare semp augusto.

Mainz, Peter Schöffer. 1473.

Folio, 364 leaves [lacking final blank], not foliated, rubricated and decorated initials. and some borders. 390 x 278 mm (text in 45 lines of double columns and 60 lines for the commentary, and with an extra line at folio 284: 'finito libro sit laus et Gloria cristo'). Eighteenth-century morocco. [22016].

Bookplates: (1) the Imperial library of St Petersburg 'Exemplum 1ᵘⁿᵈ'; (2) Bibliotheca Suchtelen [Count Suchtelen, 1751–1836]; (3) ex libris Roy Dobbin.

Annotations: sparse, marginal throughout the text.

Peter Schöffer and his father-in-law, Johann Fust, worked with Gutenberg in Mainz but the three fell out. Fust sold printed books at the same price as manuscripts. This nearly cost him his life. For, noticing that every copy was identical to the smallest detail, a critic exclaimed: 'here is the Devil's work'. Fust emphasised that the book, although appearing to be in manuscript, had not been created with the use of reed, stylus or quill but with the 'heads of type-letters'. But he had to make a hasty escape before, charged with sorcery, he and his books were burned. This explains the disclaimer in Schöffer's colophon. A bookseller's description for this copy, loosely inserted, confirms

that it was printed with type used for the 36-line Bible. Best known for the *Confessions* written in 397 AD and their whimsical quote: 'Lord, make me chaste, but not yet', Augustine wrote *De civitate Dei* after the sacking of Rome (August 410 AD) in answer to the earlier claim from Ammianus Marcellinus (c. 325–c. 391 AD) that pagan Rome was in decline. Augustine agreed that the state could only survive if pervaded by Christian ideals; and he describes theology in relation to the history of mankind and God's influences on the world.

LUCIUS MESTRIUS PLUTARCHUS (45–120 AD). [*Vitœ*].

[Incipit] Thesei vita per lapum Florentinum ex Plurarcho Græcoin Latinum versa.

[Colophon] Virorum illustrium uitæ ex Plutarcho græco in latinum uersæ solertiq; cura emendatæ sœliciter explicuit Nicolaum Ienson Gallicum Venetiis impressæ. M.cccc.lxxviii. die. Ii. Ianuarii.

Venice, Nicolas Jenson. 1478.

Folio, 456 leaves [lacking folio 1, blank], foliated as 455 [1] in a later hand (with errors corrected from an earlier count), red initials supplied in manuscript. 420 x 268 mm. Nineteenth-century half-calf with marbled paper boards, hinges worn and weak. [7235].

Annotated: (1) headers added to each leaf; (2) various marginal notes in Latin with occasional cartoons, unattributed.

Nicolas Jenson (1420–80), master of the French royal mint, went to Mainz in 1458 at the suggestion of Charles VII (1403–61) to learn the art of printing with moveable type. The plan was for him to return to Paris and set up a printer's workshop but the King died and Jenson is next heard of in Venice where he introduced a new typeface based on Caroline calligraphy, in preference to Gothic script. These changes were adopted by Aldus Manutius. Jenson and Aldine type were designed by Francesco Griffo (1450–1518) and copied by Claude Garamond (1480–1561). Their letter-forms persisted for two centuries and some were revived in the twentieth century. Plutarch observed at first hand eleven Roman emperors who he compared for their morality. He had experience of Greek and Roman society and considered the parallel lives of individual statesmen leaning more on the historical than ethical aspects of their lives. A Latin printed edition, *Vitæ parallelæ*, edited by Giovanni Antonio Campano (1429–77), first appeared in 1470. The work may have served as a sourcebook for Renaissance writers including William Shakespeare (1564–1616).

ABOVE AND RIGHT: Marginal annotations from Plutarch's *Vitæ* (1478)

[GUILLAUME GUERSON] (fifteenth century). [*Instruction de bien dancer*].

[Incipit] Sensuit lart et instruction de bien dancer.

[Colophon] Le sinnissent les regles de däcer toutes däces avecqs celles regles sont notees pour jouer a tous instrumens nouellement imprimees a Paris aumont sainct hylaire: par Michiel tholouze alenseigne de la come du cerf.

Paris, Michiel Tholouze. c. 1490.

Quarto, 12 leaves, not paginated, text and music on a four-line stave, red and black type, and two woodcuts. Bound-in woodcut with manuscript: 'La noble et excellente entrée du Roy notre sire en la bille de Florence qui fut le xvii.e jour de novembre cccc.iiii.xxxx.iiii … imprime en Paris en anno dm iiio cccco: lxxxviiio'. 190 x 135 mm. Twentieth-century half-morocco with paper boards. [21430].

Annotated: (1) 19 line preface in pseudo-contemporary English: The preface to ye reders … The diligence that o[ur] forfathers have always plide to pleasure there posterite as it doth apeare manye ways … or also alle ye note welle: vale; (2) 1488 (added to colophon).

This is the only known copy of the earliest printed book on dancing. It came to the College with books bequeathed by the Marquis of Dorchester. A facsimile was published by the College in 1936. Originally bound with another item, *Instruction de bien dancer* escaped attention and did not appear in the 1664 Salusbury catalogue. The printing of musical notation in the fifteenth century was problematic since the lines of the stave and the notes had each to be aligned. Fust and Schöffer left blank space for both to be inserted by hand (*Psalterium* 1457). In time, musical notes were printed from punches, the lines of the stave being filled in manually (*Collectorium super magnificat*, 1473). Movable musical types were used in *Missale herbipolense* (1481). A woodblock with both elements printed was used by Nicolaus Burtius (c.1450–1518: *Musices opusculum*, 1487). Wynken de Worde (1455–1534) printed the first book with music in England (*The polychronicon of Ralph Higden*, 1495). In *Instruction de bien dancer*, the red text and stave lines are printed and the black notes and further text added as a second step.

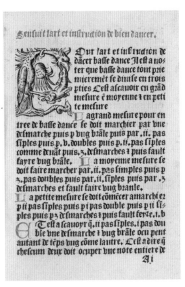

Incipit and musical notation from Guerson's *Instruction de bien dancer* (c. 1490)

SIXTEENTH CENTURY

JOANNES DE KETHAM [Kirchheim] (fifteenth century). [*Fasciculus medicinæ*].

[Incipit] Incipit fasciculus medicine compositus p[er] excellentissimus artium ac medicine doctorem: dominus Ioannem de Ketham Alamanum tractans de anathomia & diuersis infirmitatibus … Necnon anathomia Mundini.

[Colophon] Impressum Venetijs per Joannem & Gregorius de Gregoriis fratres. Anno domini M.cccc. die xxviij Marti.

Venice, Johannes and Gregorius de Gregorius. 1500.

Folio. 34 leaves, not foliated, including 10 full-page woodcuts [nine are from woodblocks re-used from the 1494 edition, and with the anatomy class from 1495], rubricated and with woodcut initials. 307 x 215 mm. Twentieth-century limp vellum. [54541].

Annotated: sixteenth century in various hands, unattributed.

It took time for the observation of natural phenomena – Francis Bacon's (1561–1626) book of nature – to take precedence over faithful rehearsal of classical dogma, and for illustration of original scientific observation by artists and skilled draughtsmen directly to depict structure based on specimens that the writer of a scientific book had examined. Derived from various manuscripts dating from the thirteenth century, Ketham's book was first printed in 1491 (Venice). Fourteen editions appeared before 1523. The book is important for containing the first medical woodcut illustrations, including the depiction of supposed dissections. The figures are: (1) Petrus de Montagnana in his study; (2) urine consultation; (3) flask wheel and description of the four humours of the body; (4) vein man; (5) zodiac man;

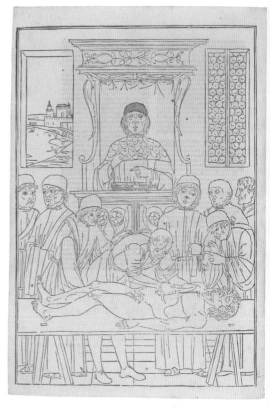

(6) pregnant woman; (7) wound man; (8) disease man; (9) visit to the plague patient; and (10) anatomy class.

OPPOSITE: Leonard Fuchs (1501–66), with attention from a bookworm, from *Herbal* (1542) ABOVE: The anatomy class from Ketham's *Fasciculus medicinæ* (1500)

MARCUS TULLIUS CICERO (106–43 BC).
[Opera].

[Incipit] M.T. Ciceronis opera. Ex Petri Victorii codicibus maxima ex parte descripta, viri docti et in recensendis authoris huius scriptis cauti & perdiligentis: quem nos industria, quanta potuimus, co[n]sequuti, quasdam orationes redintegratas, tres libros de legibvs multo quàm antea meliores, & reliquias de commentariis qui de repvblica inscripti erant, magno labore collectas vndique, descriptásque libris, vobis exhibemus. Eiusdem Victorii explicationes suarum in Ciceronem castigationum. Index rerum et verborum.

Paris, Robert Estienne. 1539.

Folio; two volumes, 540 and 499 leaves, paginated as [16] 640 [8] 416: and 1–78, 81–158 [102] 288 452. 385 x 250 mm. Volume 1, twentieth-century calf (rebacked); Volume 2, contemporary blind-tooled calf (rebacked) with remains of clasps, by John Reynes; and fore-edge lettering. [10549/50].

Inserted: stamp of C.E. Smart bookbinding restoration, Catford SE6, May 1950.

Annotated: extensive marginal notes in Latin and cartoons by John Dee.

John Dee (1527–1608) combined scholarship with a presence in public life. His depiction by Henry Gillard Glindoni (1852–1913) as 'John Dee performing an experiment before Queen Elizabeth I' included images of Edward Kelley (1555–97: alchemist and medium), Walter Raleigh (c.1552–1618) and Lord Burghley (1520–98). Dee left for a continental tour in 1583 taking 800 items from his library in a cart. In his absence, Nicholas Saunder (and others) pillaged the remaining library, removing traces of Dee's ownership as best they could. Most books had been marked with Dee's name signed backwards; and with small motifs such as the ship in full sail in this copy of Cicero, or with fore-edge markings, that reveal the provenance. The Cicero came as part of the Marquis of Dorchester's bequest and may have found its way to that library from Nicholas Saunder. Volume 2 is bound by John Reynes (d.1545), the original binding of Volume 1 having been discarded at some point. A copy of Paulus de Middelburgo's (1446–1534) *De recta paschæ* (1513) from Reynes' workshop was presented to Henry VIII (1491–1547) by Thomas Linacre, and decorated with Reynes' trademark, the Royal Arms and a Tudor rose. The Cicero is stamped with roll-tools that include 'JR' and his thistle, bee, bird, flowers and hound. The house of Estienne opened in 1502 with Henri's son Robert (1503–59) succeeding to the business in 1524. Robert was required by King François I (1494–1547) to donate one copy of each publication, thereby establishing the first copyright library. The *Opera* describe ancient Rome and include Cicero's speeches (forensic and otherwise), correspondence and his political and philosophical writings (some translated and adapted from others). Opposition to Mark Antony (83–30 BC) precipitated events that led, eventually, to Cicero's assassination.

ABOVE: Annotations by John Dee (1527–1608) in Cicero's *Opera* (1539)
OPPOSITE: Binding by John Reynes (d. 1545), Cicero's *Opera*, Volume 2

LEONHARD FUCHS (1501–66). [Herbal].

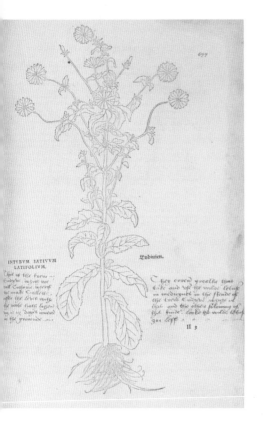

Woodcut of broad-leaved endive from Fuchs' *Herbal* (1542). The annotations advocate the use of true endive over lettuce for medicinal purposes.

De historia stirpium commentarii insignes, maximus impensis et vigiliis elaborati adiectis earvndem vivis plvsqvam quingentis imaginibus, nunquam antea ad natura imitationem artificiosius effictis & expressis, Leonharto Fvchsio medico hac nostra ætate longe clarissimo autore … etc.

Basle, Michael Isingrin. 1542.

Folio, 463 leaves, paginated as [28] 896 [2], including 511 full page woodcuts and one half-page, portraits of Leonhard Fuchs, and of Heinricus Füllmauer (c.1505–46) and Albertus Meyer (n.d.) [illustrators] and Veit Rudolph Speckle (n.d.) [block-cutter]. 365 x 235 mm. Twentieth-century morocco with blind-tooling. [21034].

Inscribed: (1) Jos[eph] Cobbe (twice); (2) contemporary, unattributed.

Annotated: scattered throughout in margins of the text and on some illustrations.

This, the most splendid of all herbals, is arranged alphabetically and marks a transition from the origins of medical botany to the enlightenment of Carl Linnaeus (1707–78: *Species plantarum*, 1753). For each plant Fuchs gives the Greek, Latin, German and occasionally Arabic names; a botanical description, mostly copied from Hieronymus Bock (1498–1554) and Pedanius Dioscorides (40–90 AD); where it grows; the time of flowering; its 'temperament' according to the Hippocratic humoral system of hot, cold, dry and wet; and its medicinal uses. The fine lines of the woodcut illustrations may lack floral detail but provide clarity and accuracy and enable each plant to be identified at species level. Fuchs complained about his medical colleagues: 'one can scarcely find one in a hundred who has an accurate knowledge of even a few plants'. He describes 400 German and 100 foreign plants, including a first description and illustration of maize, pumpkin, French marigold, chili peppers and aubergines brought in from the New World.

This, the most splendid of all herbals . . . marks a transition from the origins of medical botany to the enlightenment of Carl Linnaeus.

THOMAS RAYNALDE
(sixteenth century). [The birth of mankind].

The byrth of mankind, otherwise named the womans booke newly set furth, corrected and augmented. Whole contents ye maye rede in the table of the booke, and most plainly in the prologue. By Thomas Raynold phusition. Anno MDxlv.

[Colophon] ... And thus here I make an ende of this fourth and last booke. Imprinted at London by Tho. Ray.

London, Thomas Raynald. 1545.

Quarto, 176 leaves, foliated as [22] 148 but with many errors beyond leaf 41, woodcut title border, and two anatomical and seventeen birth figures on six engraved plates printed on four leaves. 115 x 75 mm. Nineteenth-century morocco, hinges worn and weak. [20159].

Inscribed: (1) Jn° Westbrook 3/ d. 1711; (2) Geo Putland; (3) Anna Akehurst her booke.

Annotated: BM copy has a leaf before title with coat of arms on *recto* and physician at [?] on the *verso*.

This is a translation from Latin of a popular book on midwifery illustrated with woodcuts, *Der swangern frauwen und hebammen roszgarten* (1513) by Eucharius Rösslin (1470–1526). The text and original figures of the child *in utero* were copied from a sixth-century Moschion manuscript itself based on the work of Soranus of Ephesus (98–138 AD). The first English translation, by Richard Jona[e]s (n.d.) was published in 1540. The 1545 edition added an extensive prologue by Thomas Raynalde, to whom the authorship was then assigned. This was reprinted many times up to 1654. Whereas Rösslin wrote from the perspective of the midwife, Raynalde offered a general text addressed to the mother adding remedies for the treatment of fertility to the existing text on pregnancy, birth and infant care. Thomas Raynalde may

be Thos. Raynalde, Fellow of Merton College, Oxford, who, through the influence of John Chambre (1470–1549), physician to Henry VIII, became chaplain to Lady Jane Seymour (1508–37). He is not to be confused with Thomas Raynald (n.d.: Tho. Ray.) who printed the first three editions of the book and, adding to the confusion, was also a physician. Anatomical illustrations were added to the birth figures in 1545, being the first book in English to contain copper plates. These are plagiarised from Vesalius (1514–64: *De fabrica* etc., 1543). The diagrams of foetal positions were later reused in the book of the English midwife, Jane Sharp's (n.d.), *The midwives book* (1671), who wrote:

women cannot attain so rarely to the knowledge of things as men may, who are bred up in universities ... but ... the art of midwifery [as] even the best learned men will grant ... they are forced to borrow from us the very name they practice by – man-midwives.

Raynalde offered a general text addressed to the mother adding remedies for the treatment of fertility to the existing text on pregnancy, birth and infant care.

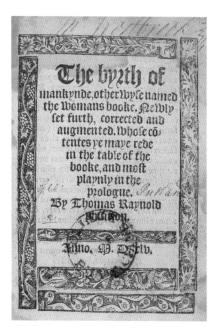

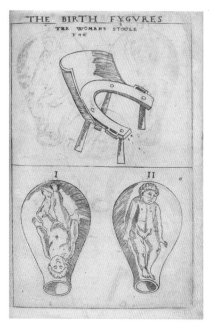

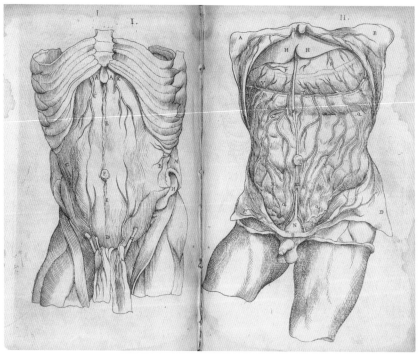

Title page, birth figures and anatomy figures from Raynalde's *The birth of mankind* (1545)

JEAN FERNEL (1497–1558). [*De naturali parte medicinæ*].

De naturali parte medicinæ libri septem
Ioanne Fernelio ambianate autore: Mendis
quamplurimis, incuria prætermiæis, præsertim
in dictionibus Græcis, expurgati. index insuper
tertia plus ferè parte locupletior redditus.

Venice, Jean Gryphe. 1547.

Octavo, 287 leaves, foliated as [blank] [22] [2
blanks] 260 [2 blanks], printed in italics apart
from the marginal notes, engraved initials. 160 x
107 mm. Nineteenth-century half-morocco with
marbled paper boards, hinges worn and now in sad
condition. [299].

Bookplate: Ex libris D. Lloyd Roberts MB FRCP
Manchester 1911.

Inscribed: Pravia Folerij on lower edge.

Annotated: unattributed.

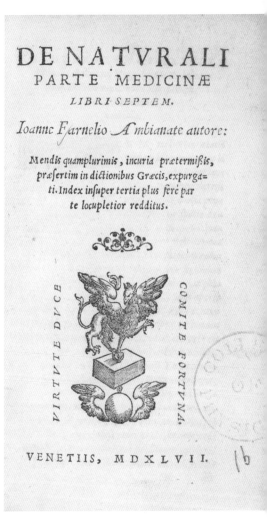

Fernel started work on *De naturali* etc., in 1538 and the book was first published in 1542 but only two copies survive outside France (one in the Hunterian Library, Glasgow). It has no illustrations because Fernel considered these to be a distraction from the direct study of dissections. Later, *De naturali* etc., was incorporated as the first part of Fernel's general book, *Medicina* (1554). Here, Fernel coins the term 'physiologia' (and, later, 'pathologia'), including the study of the mind and brain. He describes the central canal of the spinal cord and gives a first hint of reflex action or non-voluntary movement. Not yet adopting a classification based on physiological systems, Fernel retains the principles of the four humours and qualities. In considering the internal causes of disease, he abandons magic and superstition as forces in illness and distinguishes structure and function. (Sir) Charles Sherrington (1857–1952) raised awareness of Fernel, assessed his contributions in the context of his contemporaries and immediate successors, and produced a fine biography and bibliography of his writings (*The endeavour of Jean Fernel*, 1946).

JOHN CAIUS (1510–73). [The sweating sicknesse].

A boke, or counseill against the disease commonly called the sweate, or sweatyng sicknesse. Made by Jhon Caius Doctour in physicke. Very neccessary for everye personne, and muche requisite to be had in the hands of al sortes, for their better instruction, preparacion and defence, against the soubdein comyng, and fearful assaultyng of the same disease.

[Colophon] Imprinted at London, by Richard Grafton Printer to the kynges maiestie. Anno. Do. 1552. Cum privilegio ad impris mendum folum.

London, Richard Grafton. 1552.

Octavo, 40 leaves: foliated (with errors) as 39 [1], woodcut title border and complex allegorical printer's device on final leaf. 140 x 95 mm. Nineteenth-century morocco. [16834].

Bookplate: From the library of D. Lloyd Roberts MD FRCP Ravenswood Broughton Park Manchester.

Annotated: extensive marginal markings.

Unlike Vesalius, John Caius (Kaye), did not challenge the Galenic principles of medicine. He was concerned that the work of Greek and Roman physicians had not been faithfully translated and he travelled in search of original manuscripts and printed books. After his death, a catalogue of Caius' library was published (*Historia Cantabrigiensis,* 1574). Some of these books remain in the College library. Caius' treatise on sweating sickness was the

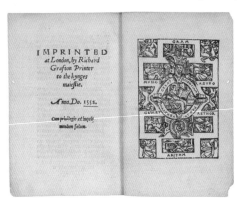

first book published in England devoted to a single disease. The sweating sickness of 1551 was milder than that of 1528. The epidemic began at Shrewsbury on 15 April, with bad odours arising from the banks of the Severn, and spread rapidly along the river and from there to the south-east – 'wheresoever the winds wafted the stinking mists'. Victims became delirious and might die within hours. People fled, or isolated themselves, but to no avail. There were 900 deaths in London, where businesses closed. Named 'stu[o]p-gallant', the illness claimed the lives of young and old, rich and poor, nobility and peasantry. But it was said that sickness spared foreigners and followed the English wherever they took refuge. Caius attributed this to intemperance and the immoderate use of beer; or a constitutional 'opportunity'. The King, managing affairs from Hampton Court, advised prayer in order to avert the displeasure of Almighty God, who he perceived to have visited the realm with the extreme plague of sudden death. The epidemic subsided by September and no further episodes of that particular illness seem to have occurred.

Caius' treatise on sweating sickness was the first book published in England devoted to a single disease.

ABOVE: Colophon and printer's allegorical device depicting the arts and sciences from Caius' *The sweating sickness* (1552)

GABRIELE FALLOPPIO
(1523–62). [*Opera*].

Opera quae adhuc extant omnia in unum congesta & in medicinæ studiosorum gratiam nunc primum tali ordine excusa.

Frankfurt, Andreas Wechel. 1584.

Folio, 446 leaves, paginated as [12] 848 [32]. 330 x 200 mm. Contemporary calf with blind-tooling. [14138].

Inserted: Printed shelf-label '14' typical of books saved from the Great Fire, although in the 1660 catalogue the book has the shelf mark 'E.3.G'.

Inscribed: Lancelot Browne.

Annotated: (1) Notes on two preliminary leaves (probably in Browne's hand), one providing an index, and with the shelf-label for Christopher Merrett's catalogue; (2) Lancelot Browne; (3) William Harvey's WH monogram and Greek Δ [for *demonstratio*], mainly at pages 303–97 in the section *De metallis seu fossilibus*.

Accused of human vivisection, Gabriele Fallopius (1523–62) was a prominent Italian anatomist in Padua who described the chorda tympani and semi-circular canals; several cranial nerves (adding the trochlear); the cerebral vasculature, including the way in which vessels vary their diameter and hence the flow of blood; the musculature of many parts; and the genital tracts of women and men (for which he is best remembered). These descriptions, and the remainder of Fallopius' writings, were edited for publication after his death and gathered in the *Opera*; but his illustrated anatomical work, mentioned as close to completion, never materialised. Turning the pages of *Opera* etc., the reader is handling the copy that William Harvey owned and annotated; and which, on 3 September 1666, Christopher Merrett grabbed from the College premises at Amen Corner and ran down Ave Maria Lane as the flames closed behind him on the burning City of London. Harvey's writing is notoriously indecipherable. In 1877 the manuscript of his lecture notes, *Praelectiones* (1616), which contained comments on the circulation of the blood, was discovered in the Sloane papers secreted in the British Museum. But even the efforts of Joseph Payne (1840–1910) and (Sir) Norman Moore, and an expert from the British Museum, Edward Scott (n.d.), failed fully to decipher the annotations. In modern times, the great expert on Harvey's handwriting was Gweneth Whitteridge (1910–93).

William Harvey's annotations in his copy of Falloppio's *Opera* (1584)

EXERCITATIO

ANATOMICA DE

MOTV CORDIS ET SAN-
GVINIS IN ANIMALI-
BVS,

GVILIELMI HARVEI ANGLI,

Medici Regii, & Professoris Anatomiæ in Col-
legio Medicorum Londinensi.

FRANCOFVRTI,
Sumptibus GVILIELMI FITZERI,
ANNO M. DC. XXVIII.

SEVENTEENTH CENTURY

JOSEPHUS STRUTHIUS (1510–68).
[The art of the pulse].

Ars sphygmica seu pulsuum doctrina ... libris V conscripta, & iam primum aucta. Accessit Hieronymi Capivaccei de pulsibus elegans tractatus: & Caspari Bauhini Introductio pulsuum synopsin continens.

Basle, Ludovici Koenigs. 1602.

Octavo, 263 leaves, paginated as [20] 23 [5] 460 [18], various woodcut figures, including pulse waves, in the text; and folding table. 155 x 100 mm. Nineteenth-century half-calf with marbled paper boards, worn with crude repairs to inner hinges. [38060].

Bookplates: (1) E Bibliotheca Reverendi Doctissimique viri Edwardi Waple STB Ecclesiæ Sti. Sepulchri London. Vicarii. MDCCXII; (2) Ex libris D.A.H. Moses MC; (3) The Evan Bedford Library of Cardiology presented to the Royal College of Physicians of London by Dr Evan Bedford CBE FRCP May 1971.

Stamped: Sion College sold by order of the president and governors 1938.

Inscribed: D Evan Bedford.

Struthius was physician to Polish kings and sometime mayor of Poznań. Opposed to but respectful of the views of Galen and Avicenna, Struthius suggested a method for quantitative estimation of blood pressure by displacement of graded weights, and he provided the first study of the pulse illustrated in graphic form. Struthius described vasomotor nerves that alter the calibre of blood vessels. First published in 1555 by Johannes Oporinus (1507–68) of Basle, this book was used by Harvey in his work on the circulation of the blood but ignored by most standard historians of medicine, including Harvey's biographers, (Sir) D'Arcy Power (1855–1941) and (Sir)

Geoffrey Keynes (1887–1982). Robert Burton (1577–1640) was more attentive in *The anatomy of melancholy* (1621) quoting from *Ars syphygmica*: 'touch clearly perceives not only the beat of the artery but also its expansion ... passions of the mind may be discovered by the pulse'. Struthius pointed out that lying might be detected by observations of the pulse. Evan Bedford (1898–1978) left the College about a thousand books and pamphlets on cardiology, catalogued and annotated with respect to the provenance and significance for heart disease. These are shelved in a dedicated space within the Dorchester Library. A printed catalogue was prepared in 1978.

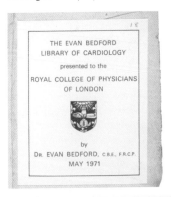

OPPOSITE: Harvey's *De motu cordis* (1628), arguably the most important book in the history of medicine
ABOVE: Graphic representation of the pulse from Struthius' *The art of the pulse* (1602)

THOMAS VICARY (1490–1561).
[The English man's treasure].

The English mans treasure with the true anatomie of mans bodie: compiled by that excellent chirurgion, M Thomas Vicary esquire, Sergeant Chirurgion to King Henry the 8. To King Edward the 6. To Queen Marie, and to our late Soveraigne ladie Queene Elizabeth. And also Chirurgion to Saint Bartholomewes Hospitall ... Also the rare treasure of the English bathes: written by William Turner, Doctor in Physicke.

London, Thomas Creede. 1613.

Quarto, 117 leaves, paginated as [8] 224 [10] (lacking 41-8)] with illustration of a human skeleton [Bound-in at the end, the title page for The description of a maske as presented in the banqueting room at Whitehall on Saint Stephens night, at the marriage of the Right Honorable the Earle of Somerset; and the right noble the Lady Frances Howard, written by Thomas Campion etc., 1614]. 172 x 134 mm. Twentieth-century cloth. [16093].

Inscribed: (1) unattributed, with figures; (2) Robt Moss at the Cross Keyes Woodstreet etc.

Annotated: marginal chalk marks.

Thomas Vicary, Master of the Barber-Surgeons' Company, was 'a meane practiser in Maidstone … that had gayned his knowledge by experience, untill the King advanced him for curing his sore legge' after which he became the Royal Sergeant-Surgeon. Latin persisted in medical texts written by physicians to the end of the seventeenth century, perhaps as a sign of superiority over surgeons, who preferred to write in the vernacular. This is the first anatomy written in English. Joseph Payne showed that it is derivative, being a shortened version of a fourteenth-century manuscript written in Middle English by an anonymous London surgeon, who himself had copied the work of earlier writers, probably including Guido Lanfranc and Henri de Mondeville. The printed text may have started as *A treasure for Englishmen*

containing the anatomie of man's body and was closely associated with St Bartholomew's Hospital but with Vicary designated as author (1548; of which no surviving copy is known). This was revised as *A profitable treatise of the anatomy of man's body* (1577: two copies survive); and *The Englishmans treasure; with the true anatomy of mans bodie* etc. (1586 and subsequent editions). The 1613 edition is expanded with authorship by Vicary, Turner, Bremer and G.E. There is a pharmacopoeia – 'Heeraftere followeth sundry waters and medicines, meete for physicke, and chyurgerie, as also oyntments and plaisters'; 'A medicine for the plague, and sickness of the soule'; and the book ends with a prayer.

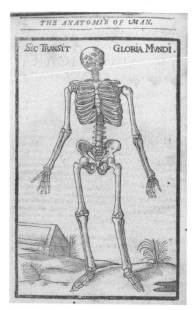

The human skeleton from Vicary's *The English man's treasure* (1613)

[ANON]. [London pharmacopoeia].

Pharmacopoeia Londinensis in qua medicamenta antiqua et nova usitatissima sedulò collecta accuratissimé examinata, quotidiana experientia confirmata describuntur. Opera medicorum Collegii Londinensis. Ex serenissimi regis mandato cum R M Privilegio.

London, Edward Griffin. 1618.

Folio, 109 leaves, paginated as [16] 184, [18], woodcut title-border. 267 x 185 mm. Later calf with blind-tooling. [18370].

Annotated: (1) This is the first edition of the Pharmacopoeia published May 7th 1618 – the second edition was also published in 1618 on the 7th of December. JB Sedgwick; (2) throughout the text [possibly Middleton Massey, and others].

First suggested in 1585, the College was prompted to publish its pharmacopoeia as a means of controlling the production and sale of compound medicines by the apothecaries. The College relied heavily on the most recent edition of the Nuremberg *Pharmacopoeia Augustana* (1613), itself based on the *Pharmacorum omnium* (1546) of Valerius Cordus (1515–44), who had compiled a list of the compound medicines in use over the previous 1500 years. Superficially a redacted version, and plagiarised both with respect to the content and formatting of the text, the book describes a considerable number of new compounds among the 712 medicines. Some had first been identified by Galen, a large number by Mesue (the Persian physician Yūhannā Ibn Māsawayh, c. 777–857 AD), a few by Avicenna, and others by various physicians. The only fellows of the College who contributed formulae were Thomas Moundeford (1550–1630) and Theodore de Mayerne (1573–1655). We read of herbs, resins, syrups, lohochs, electuaries, troches, unguents, robs and oxymels, even the flesh of vipers, earthworms and incinerated swallows as receipts to cure all poisonings and protect from plagues and pestilence. There is nothing on illness since the College did not wish the apothecaries to know how to treat their patients and levy fees. A second edition with correct spelling, 250 more medicines and more than 300 extra ingredients appeared in November 1618. Nicholas Culpeper wrote an unauthorised translation, *A physical directory or translation of the London dispensatory* (1649), adding all the diseases that the medicines and simples treated. He accused the College of Physicians of being papists because they resisted the vernacular in medicine. Successive editions appeared prior to publication of the *British pharmacopoeia* (1864).

Annotation by J. B. Sedgwick describing editions of the *London pharmacopoeia* (1618)

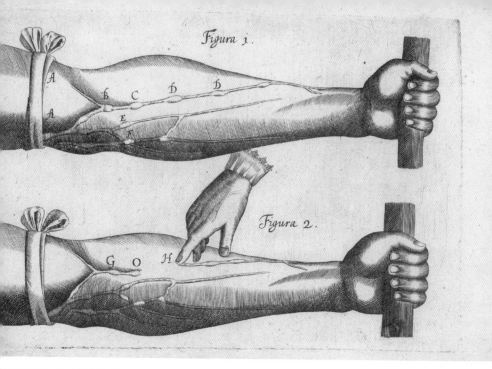

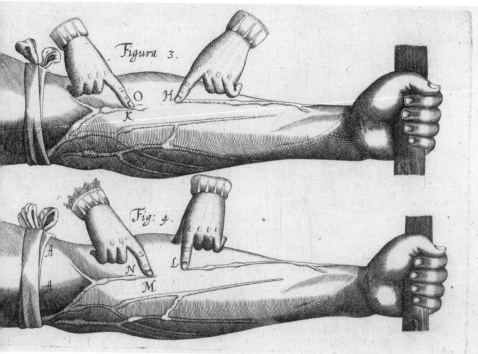

Venous sinuses and the circulation of the blood, depicted in the four figures from Harvey's *De motu cordis* (1628)

WILLIAM HARVEY (1578–1657).
[De motu cordis].

Exercitatio anatomica de motu cordis et sanguinis in animalibus.

Frankfurt, William Fitzer. 1628.

Quarto, 36 leaves, paginated as 72 with four engraved figures on two plates (between 50–51 and 56–57) [leaf 2, pp 3–4, the dedication is from the 1639 edition; the errata and final blank, leaves 37 and 38, are lacking; paper defect affecting text of leaf 8, pp 15–16; every leaf, apart from leaf 2, strengthened with tissue paper]. 200 x 145 mm. Twentieth-century morocco with blind-tooling. [22888].

Stamped with his coat of arms, inscribed and annotated, identifying errata throughout the text, by Robert Nesbitt, 1789.

Circulation of the blood had been anticipated by Realdo Colombo (1516–59: *De re anatomica* 1559); an Arab physician, Ibn Al-Nafis (1213–88); Michael Servetus (c.1511–53: *Christianismi restitutio,* 1553); Josephus Struthius (*Ars syphygmica* etc., 1555); Andrea Cesalpino (1519–1603: *Quaestionum peripateticarum,* 1571); and Fabricius ab Aquapendente (1537–1619: *De venarum ostiolis,* 1603). But where others speculated, Harvey experimented. His book was criticised and Harvey's reputation as a physician not immediately enhanced. He remained silent but replied in a riposte only to Jean Riolan (1577–1657), apparently the one critic with sufficient stature to deserve a rebuttal (*De circulatione sanguinis,* 1649). Why Harvey chose the Englishman, Fitzer, to publish his book in Frankfurt has been much debated. The best guess is that Fitzer knew Robert Fludd (1574–1637), who had trained with Harvey in Padua. Fludd's books were published by Johann Theodor de Bry (1561–1626) and the business in Frankfurt was bought by Fitzer when de Bry died. This was unfortunate since, given the distance, Harvey probably never saw proofs of his book. When it became clear that there were many errors, Harvey prepared an extra two leaves, present in a minority of copies, one of which lists the 126 corrections. Presumably Robert Nesbitt had access to these errata given the corrections he has made; but some seem to be his own emendations. The publisher also did not serve posterity well by printing the book on paper that has not lasted. Most copies are very brittle and have had to undergo extensive preservation to prevent crumbling of the leaves. Later editions of *De motu cordis,* published in several languages, are much rarer than the 1628 Frankfurt imprint, of which sixty-one copies are now known.

Where others speculated, Harvey experimented. His book was criticised and Harvey's reputation as a physician not immediately enhanced.

[ANON]. [The plague].

Certain necessary direction, as well for the cure of the plague, as for preventing the infection; with many easie medicines of small charge, very profitable to his Maiesties subjects set downe by the Colledge of Physicians by the Kings Maiesties speciall command. With sundry orders thought meet by his Majestie, and his Privie Councell, to be carefully executed for prevention of the plague. Also certaine select statutes commanded by His Majestie to be put in execution by all justices, and other officers of the peace throughout the Realme; together with His Majesties proclamation for further direction therein: and a decree in Starre-Chamber, concerning buildings and in-mates.

London, Robert Barker. 1636.

Quarto, 72 leaves, not paginated, with decorated initials, Royal arms on title page (verso) and some additional woodcuts. 170 x 130 mm. Bound with seven eighteenth-century pamphlets, twentieth-century half-calf with buckram boards. [22559-1].

Inscribed: (a list of the contents) 1. Certain necessary directions as well for the cure of the plague, as for preventing the infection. By the College of Physicians. London 1636. 4to. 2. Febrifugum Magnum: or common water the best cure for fevers. By John Hancocke. 6th edition. London 1723. 3. Siris. By Bp Berkley. 2d edit. London 1774. 4. Authentic narrative of the success of tar water. By Thos. Prior. London 1726. 5. A practical dissertation on drowning. London. 1746. 6. Relief from accidental death. Derby. 7. Friendly admonition to the drinkers of gin &c. by Stephen Hales. 4th edition. London 1751. 8. Dissertatio medica in auguralis. Jac: Barton. Lugdani Batavorum 1788.

Epidemics of the plague – manifesting as fever, buboes, carbuncles and death – occurred at regular intervals during the first half of the seventeenth century: in 1603 (38,000 deaths), 1611 (11,785 deaths), 1625 (35,417 deaths), 1630 (1317 deaths), 1636 (13,624 deaths) and others up to the Great Plague of London in 1665–6 (70,596 deaths). Plague accounted for approximately 50 per cent of all deaths in these years. The highest density in 1636 was suburban, with fewer infected within the City walls. William Heberden (1710–1801) claimed that it started in Whitechapel. People left the City, including many physicians who preceded their patients in the hurry to avoid contamination. Eleven persons were committed to Newgate Prison for the irresponsibility of escorting Samuel Underhill, a trumpeter, by night to his grave at Shoreditch with trumpets blaring and swords drawn. The College was inconvenienced in 1625 and 1630 and suspended much of its business. In 1631, the plague was around Amen Corner, and meetings were held at the President's house in Warwick Court. The College of Physicians advised the Lord Mayor in 1625; prepared regulations for the Privy Council in 1630; and, in 1636, issued 'necessary directions', largely rehearsing those from 1625. The causes were overcrowding and 'nuisances' . . . 'those who died of the plague were buried within the City, and some of the graveyards were so full that partially decomposed bodies were taken up to make room for fresh interments'.

People left the City, including many physicians who preceded their patients in the hurry to avoid contamination.

CERTAIN

necessary Directions as-
well for the Cure of the
Plague, as for preuenting
the Infection;

With many easie Medicines of small charge, very pro-
fitable to his Maiesties Subiects,

Set downe by the Colledge of Physicians at the
Kings MAIESTIES speciall command;

With sundry Orders thought meet by his Maiestie, and his
Priuie Councell, to be put in execution for preuention
of the Plague.

Also certaine select Statutes commanded
by His Maiestie to be put in execution by all
Iustices, and other officers of the Peace
throughout the Realme;

Together with His Maiesties Proclamation for further
direction therein : and a Decree in Starre-Chamber, concerning buildings and In-mates.

¶ Imprinted at London by ROBERT
BARKER, Printer to the Kings most Excellent
MAIESTIE: And by the Assignes of
IOHN BILL. 1636.

THOMAS BROWNE (1605–82).
Religio medici.

Religio medici.

London, Andrew Crooke. 1642.

Octavo, 96 leaves, paginated as [2] 190, engraved title page [with 'Religio medici à coclo salus' (printed obliquely on a falling angel)]. 140 x 85 mm. Contemporary sheep, lacking spine, boards and text block detached. [12672].

Inscribed (1): F Hosier (twice, contemporary); (2) Religio medici &. Thomas Brown Docter of Phisick. The 2nd part begins at the 135th page. I had this peece of Docter John Simpson in exchange for natura Prodigiorum or the nature of prodigies by John Gadbury, unsigned and with marginal annotations in the same hand; (3) This is a copy of the first unauthorized edition, & is probably very scarce. A facsimile reprint was published by Elliot Stock, London 1883. May '84 WAG [William Alexander Greenhill (1814–94)].

Browne wrote in a distinctive and influential prose style. *Religio medici*, his views on religion as a physician, was written in c.1634 but not intended for publication. However, Andrew Crooke (d.1674) obtained a manuscript copy and published an unauthorised edition in 1642. The title page was engraved by Edward Marshall (1598–1674), who carved the bust on Harvey's tomb and the statue commemorating his gift of the museum. (Sir) William Osler (1849–1919) and Keynes identified another unauthorised edition also published in 1642 (but with only 159 pages) to which they assign priority on the basis that the engraved frontispiece is fresh and unworn, unlike the 190-page edition from the same year. The College has both items but the 159-page volume has the engraved frontispiece in facsimile, making direct comparison of this bibliographic detail impossible. Browne cooperated with a subsequent authorised edition (1643), and *Religio medici* went through thirteen editions in the seventeenth century, four in the eighteenth, twenty-six in the nineteenth and thirty-one in the twentieth centuries. Several collections of Browne's works were made, notably that by Osler. Arnold Chaplin, Harveian librarian, failed to secure for the College the collection made by Lloyd-Roberts and this went to the John Rylands (University) Library in Manchester. A sale catalogue of the libraries of Thomas Browne and his son Edward was printed in 1710 or 1711, and included 2377 lots classified by subject and size. This was held in the auction rooms of Thomas Ballard (n.d.), twenty-eight years after Browne's death. Only four copies of the catalogue are known.

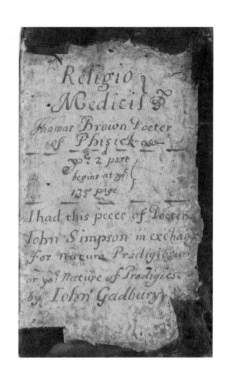

OPPOSITE: Allegorical engraved title page from Browne's *Religio medici* (1642)
RIGHT: A note on the provenance of this copy by John Gadbury
BELOW: A note by William Greenhill on the editions of *Religio medici*, probably incorrect

DANIEL WHISTLER (1619–84).
[The rickets].

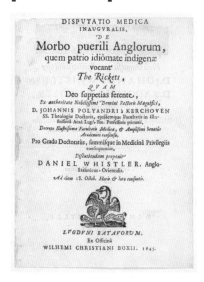

On his watch, the finances of the College ... suffered through casual financial management verging on criminality and ... embezzlement by Whistler.

Disputatio medica inauguralis de morbo puerili Anglorum, quem patrio idiômate indigenæ vocant. The Rickets.

Leyden, Wilhelm Christian Boxius. 1645.

Quarto, 8 leaves pasted onto nineteenth-century folio sheets inserted into an earlier blank-book together comprising 60 sheets, not paginated. 180 x 135 mm. Seventeenth-century calf, rebacked. [16762].

Daniel Whistler claimed that his treatise on rickets, printed in 1684 but with the same text as this medical thesis written at Leyden in 1645, preceded Francis Glisson's (1597–1677) more famous book on rickets (*De rachitide* etc., 1650). This proved correct when the copy of Whistler's thesis was discovered in the College library in 1883. Admitted to the fellowship in 1649, Whistler was subsequently Censor, Registrar, Treasurer and, 'in an evil hour', elected President in 1683. His portrait, 'in company too good for his deserts', was given by Mr Boulter (n.d.) to whom thanks were voted on 26 June 1704. Whistler took advantage of his position to defraud the College over which he presided; but in what precise manner, or to what extent, is not recorded. Posterity judges that, on his watch, the finances of the College in general, and those of the library in particular, suffered through casual financial management verging on criminality and – as it has been argued by some – embezzlement by Whistler. William Munk wrote in his *Roll* etc., that:

Dr Whistler's character will not bear examination; and it would have been well for the interests of the College had he not been admitted to some, at least, of the places of trust he was elected to fill. His manners were agreeable, and he shone particularly in society; yet it is but too evident that duty, honour, and probity weighed but lightly with him ... his duties he systematically neglected; and our Annals, especially during the latter period he held office, are in perplexing and inextricable confusion.

THOMAS WILLIS
(1621–75). *Cerebri anatome.*

Cerebri anatome: cui accessit nervorum descriptio et usus. Studio Thomæ Willis, Ex æde Christi Oxon. M.D. & in ista Celeberrima academia naturalis philosophiæ professoris Sidleiani.

London, Ja[mes] Flesher for Jo[hn] Martyn and Ja[cob] Allestry. 1664.

Octavo, 249 leaves, paginated as [40] 456 (inter-page between 106 and 107), 23 figures on 15 plates. 220 x 160 mm. Contemporary calf with gilt tooling, rebacked, and marbled edges. [16796].

Bookplate: (1) George Putland Esq; (2) (Sir Richard) Manningham.

Inscribed: (1) Geo. Putland; (2) Greek and Latin notes.

Annotated: sparsely in Greek and Latin throughout, unattributed.

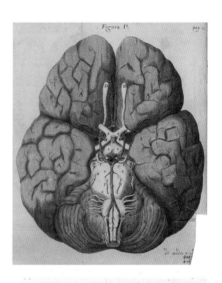

CAP. XIX. De fyftemate nervofo in genere, ubi partibus ejus (quæ funt nervi & fibræ) defignatis, totius œconomiæ animalis prospectus exhibetur.   *P.234*

N*ευρολογίας penfum,difficile licèt,utile ac jucundum eft, 235. Syftema nervofum quid,236. ejus partes primariæ funt nervi, fecundariæ funt fibræ,237. fpiritus intra nervos funt veluti aquarum rivi, in reliquo nervofo genere velut aquarum paludes & lacus, 238. aliàs ra-*

TOP: The 'circle of Willis' depicted by Christopher Wren from Willis' *Cerebri anatome* (1664), *Figura 1ª*, at E1r, page 25
ABOVE: First use of the term 'neurology' in the *Elenchus rerum* at C3r, page [29]

Famous for many reasons, *Cerebri anatome* is the definitive account of the anatomy of the nervous system, combining studies of structure and function and clinical case description. Christopher Wren was one of Willis' technical assistants and is identified with production of the images in *Cerebri anatome*. Wren's son considered that his father regretted moving on from scientific work to become an architect: 'King Charles II had done him a disservice in taking him from the pursuit of those studies, and obliging him to spend all his time in rubbish.' Wren invented a perspectograph that allowed a draftsman to trace the lines of any object or landscape. This was deployed in depicting the topography of the brain. Wren used intravenous injections through sharpened quills to inject the vessels of the brain with India ink and a preservative. H. J. R. Wing has suggested that figures 1–3 and 5–8 are by Wren and according to the British Library copy they were engraved by David Loggan (1634–92). Based on their artistry, it seems most likely that Wren drew plates I–VIII of *Cerebri anatome,* not plates IX–XIII and not the two unnumbered plates which were almost certainly an afterthought; and that he was also responsible for plates V–VIII of *De anima brutorum* (1672).

THOMAS SALUSBURY (c.1625–c.1665).
Bibliotheca Marchionis Dorcestriæ.

Bibliotheca Marchionis Dorcestriæ.

London, 1664.

Manuscript in Latin. Folio, 88 leaves (vellum), paginated as [4] 150 [22] with two additional leaves tipped-in headed Duplicia librorum exemplaria·in illustriss Marchionis Dorchestriæ catalogo extantia. 315 x 215 mm. Contemporary morocco with clasps, spine blind-stamped with the Dorchester coat of arms. [MS2000/81].

Inserted: stamp of C.E. Smart bookbinding restoration, Catford SE6, March 1952.

Annotated: indicating current holdings and with other notes in a later hand.

Books presented to the College by the Marquis of Dorchester after the Great Fire of London had been catalogued by Thomas Salusbury, who may have helped with the acquisitions.

Christopher Merrett catalogued books in the College library accumulated from 1518 to 1660, most of which were lost in the Great Fire of London. Only one copy of that catalogue survives. It seems likely that this was among items in Sloane's house at his death that went to the British Museum. Books presented to the College by the Marquis of Dorchester after the Great Fire had been catalogued by Thomas Salusbury, who may have helped with the acquisitions. These were valued at £4000. The classification is by size within the categories of *libri mathematici* (825 titles), *libri juris civilis* (192), *libri medici* (192) and *libri philogici* (576). Evidently many holdings were not listed, or were bound with another title. The handsome binding is by Samuel Mearne (1624–83), binder to King Charles II (1630–85). Estimates vary somewhat but the number of books in the College library was 1278 in 1660, reducing to 140 after the Great Fire in 1667; increasing to 3410 by 1688; 5480 in 1727; 8750 by 1740; but with attrition in 1825 when the library was in storage for several years. There was a steady increase to around 16,000 books in the mid-nineteenth century and, by 2018, roughly 3000 titles in the Dorchester Collection, 45,000 printed book titles, 12,000 printed articles and pamphlets (of which 20,000 books and 4000 pamphlets are pre-1900) and 40,000 manuscript or archival items.

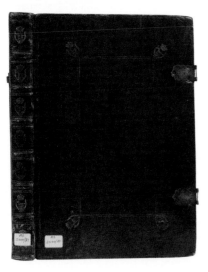

Thomas Salusbury's catalogue of books forming the Dorchester Library (1664)

MARCELLO MALPIGHI (1628–94). [*Opera omnia*].

(1) Philosophi & medici Bononiensis e Regia Societate opera omnia figuris elegantissimis in æs incisis illustrata tomis duobus comprehensa quorum catalogum sequens pagina exhibit; (2) Philosophi & medici Bononiensis e Regia Societate appendix, repetitas auctasque de ovo incubato observationes continens; (3) Philosophi & medici Bononiensis e Regia Societate operum tomus secundus.

London, Robert Littlebury. 1687; Robert Littlebury, Robert Scott, Thomas Sawbridge and George Wells. 1686.

Folio, 223 leaves, paginated as [8] 16 [4] 82 [2] 36 [6] 72 [8] 44 [4] 20 144, with engraved frontispiece, 104 full and two half-page plates. 360 x 235 mm. Contemporary calf, rebacked, now in sad condition. [17825].

Malpighi joined a group devoted to dissection and microscopy which opposed prevailing Galenic teaching. He made contributions to embryology, human and comparative anatomy of vertebrates and invertebrates (notably the silk moth, *Bombyx*), and botany. His work on the microvasculature of the ranine lungs provided evidence for the 'invisible connections' needed finally to substantiate Harvey's work on the circulation of the blood. Malpighi was active at a time when science was struggling for liberation from the constraints of religious and political censure. He suffered physical assault and periodically his working papers were destroyed. As publication in Europe became increasingly difficult, Malpighi's work after 1669 was published by the Royal Society of London, to which organisation he gave all his unpublished works. These were published as *Opera*

Allegorical frontispiece engraved by Robert White (1645–1703) from Malpighi's *Opera omnia* (1686–87)

posthuma (1696). Scrutiny of various copies of Malpighi's works printed in England suggests that his writings were bundled up in somewhat random order with the text and plates often intermingled. The copy in the College library has the two main volumes of *Opera omnia figuris elegantissimis in æs incisis illustrata tomis duobus comprehensa* separated by the appendix but it lacks the important posthumous writings. In 1695, Giovanni Lancisi (1654–1720) published an account in *Philosophical Transactions* of the autopsy on Malpighi, confirming that he had died from cerebral haemorrhage.

Francis Bernard (1627–98)

FRANCIS BERNARD (1627–98).
[Catalogue].

A catalogue of the library of the late learned Dr Francis Bernard Fellow of the College of Physicians, and Physician to S. Bartholomew's Hospital. Being a large collection of the best theological, historical, philological, medicinal and mathematical authors, in the Greek, Latin, Italian, Spanish, French, German, Dutch and German tongues, in all volumes which will be sold by auction at the doctor's late dwelling house in Little Britain: the sale to begin on Tuesday, Octob. 4. 1698. Catalogues to be sold at Mr Aylmers in Cornhil, Mr Kettilby's, and Mr Smith and Walford in S. Paul's Church-Yard, Mr Churchil, and Mr Bateman in Paternoster-Row, Mr Buckley in Fleetstreet, Mr Hartley in Holbourn, Mr Varennes and Mr. Cailloüe in the Strand, Mr Castle near Whitehal, Mr Nott's in the Pall-Mall, Mr Clements of Oxford, Mr Dawson of Cambridge, Booksellers; and at the place of sale. Price two shillings and six pence.

London, Brabazon Aylmer [and others]. 1698.

Octavo, 230 leaves, paginated as [8] 192 152 88 20. 180 x 115 mm. Original calf with blind-tooling. [22021].

Annotated: (1) with a summary of purchases; Libri theologii Fo 1, 4to 3, 8vo 14; Juridice 31, Mathematicii 40, Medicii 66; pars 2^d Philogii 1; (2) markings throughout against various items, presumably corresponding to these purchases; (3) A chapter on this very extraordinary sale will be found in John Lawler's *Book auctions in England in the 17th century* (Eliot Stock 1898) – but Lawler misdates the sale by 10 years. He gives prices of many items – twenty-two Caxtons were sold at such prices as 1s/6d. 2/s, 3/-, 3/6. Early Americana for less. Lawler reprints the whole of 'To the reader' from this volume.

Book auction catalogues in English date from the second half of the seventeenth century. The sale-catalogue of Francis Bernard's library points out that:

We must confess that being a Person who Collected his Books for Use, and not for Ostentation or Ornament, he seem'd no more solicitous about their Dress than his own; and therefore you'll find that a gilt Back or a large Margin was very seldom any inducement for him to buy.

The books are arranged by subject (theology, law, mathematics, medicine, philology, foreign language and English books on divinity and history). Within each section the ordering is by size – folio (615), quarto (1328), octavo (1965), duodecimo (576), but with no apparent system by alphabet or year of publication within these sections. Separate editions of the same book are listed randomly. Entries usually provide author and short title; some have date and place of publication. A few items are linked by brackets presumably indicating that these were to be sold together. The total number of lots (ignoring the brackets) is 15,668 including books gathered in a final collection of thirty-nine bundles. The largest subject areas are medicine and philology. Bernard's copy of Harvey's *De motu cordis*, which the annotator seems to have acquired based on a pencil mark, has Fr[ankfurt] 1627 as the date of publication. Bernard also lists an issue from 1634: a folio edition was published from Venice in 1635, but since Bernard describes the book as quarto published at Lugd[unum Batavorum] it is presumably the 1639 Leiden edition in which Harvey's text is printed paragraph-by-paragraph with separate refutations by Emilius Parisanus (n.d.) and James Primrose (d.1659). Thomas Willis *De motu naturali inorganico* (undated, but 1659) is now known only for a single copy at St John's College, Oxford: perhaps this is it. Most of Bernard's books went to John Trotter (1667–1718) and remained with that family in Scotland until 1947.

1147 Beverburg *Rud.* Collegium Anatomicum.
1148 Berretarii Tractatus de Risu, cum multis aliis, *Flor.* 160?
1149 Laudrinii *Gal.* problemata ad sanitatem & aegritudinem *Fer.* 1628.
1150 Harvey *Guil.* de Motu Cordis in Animalibus, *Fr.* 1627.
1151 Hoornbeeck *Joan.* Disp. de Phthisi, *Lugd.* 1664.
1152 Neucrantzii *Paul.* Exercit. Medica de Harengo, *Lub.* 1654
1153 Gordonus de Generatione format. Melancholia, &c. *Pat* 1621.
1154 Costaeus *Joan.* de Igneis Medicinae praesidiis, *Ven.* 1595.
1155 Salae *Ang.* tract. duo de variis Erroribus Chym.& Galeni starum cum multis aliis, *Fr.* 1649.
1156 Vander Mye *Joan.* tract. duo de Arthritide & Calculo gemino, *Hag.* 1624.

The sale of Harvey's *De motu cordis*, 1627 (*sic*)

SAMUEL GARTH (1661–1719).
[The dispensary].

The dispensary. A poem in six cantos. Quod licet, libet.

London, John Nutt. 1699.

Quarto, 43 leaves, paginated as [2] 84. 205 x 160 mm. Bound with nine other pamphlets, eighteenth-century calf, with gilt-tooling, boards detached. [13495-7].

Bookplate: George Witt.

Inscribed: From [George Witt] to the College of Physicians 1867.

Annotated: unattributed, with names inserted corresponding to places and people referred to indirectly or in disguise within the text.

Garth became involved in the dispute between the apothecaries and physicians on the dispensing of medicines and the taking of fees. In 1617, with its separation from the grocers, the College was given responsibility for regulating the activities of the apothecaries who considered that selling medicines did not need the empirical wisdom of physicians, nor restriction of their own earnings. A turf war followed in which the College decided to use its laboratory to prepare and dispense medicines at cost price to patients. The House of Lords upheld an appeal by William Rose (n.d.) against the ruling that, as an apothecary, he had 'practiced physick', concluding that the physicians seemed more concerned with protecting their privileges than the welfare of the sick. Several other pamphlets in the volume relate to this controversy. The apothecaries managed to create divisions within the College, which separated into 'Dispensarians', with whom Garth was aligned, and 'Anti-dispensarians'. In Canto I Garth writes of '… a Dome, Majestick to the Sight, and … a golden Globe plac'd high with artful Skill, [that] Seems, to the distant Sight, a gilded Pill'. He promoted the stance of the Dispensarians in his Harveian Oration (1697) and the 1699 anonymous broadsheet poem in which he used the literary tactic of masking names by insertion of hyphens. His purpose, as set out in the preface to the second edition (1699), stemmed from:

> *finding the animosities amongst the members of the College of Physicians increasing daily … I was persuaded … to endeavour to rally some of our disaffected members into a sense of their duty, who have hitherto most obstinately oppos'd all manner of union; and have continued so unreasonably refractory,* etc.

The poem was successful and went into several editions. It is considered to have been somewhat influential in the development of eighteenth-century literary style.

Then she, Alas! how long in vain have I
Aim'd at those noble ills the Fates deny:
Within this Isle for ever must I find
Disasters to distract my restless Mind.
Good *Tennison* Celestial Piety
Has rais'd his Virtues to the Sacred See.
Sommers do's sickning Equity restore,
And helpless Orphans now need weep no more.
Pembroke to *Britain* endless Blessings brings;
He spoke and Peace clap'd her Triumphant wings:
Unshaken is the Throne and safe its Lord,
Whilst *Macclesfeld* or *Ormond* wears a Sword.
The noble ardour of a Loyal Fire,
Inspires the generous breast of *Devonshire*.
Like *Leda*'s shining Sons, divinely clear,
Portland and *Iersey* deck'd in Rays appear
To Guild, by turns, the Gallick Hemisphear.
Worth in Distress is rais'd by *Montague*,
Augustus listens if *Mæcenas* sue.

And

OPPOSITE: Royal College of Physicians, Theatreum Cutlerianum: engraved frontispiece from Garth's *The dispensary* (1699) (© Alastair Compston), (see also page 9)
ABOVE: Canto II, lines 47–67, with names completed in manuscript

GEORGII EDVARDI
ORNITHOLOGIA NOVA

EIGHTEENTH CENTURY

[MIDDLETON MASSEY] (1678–1743).
[Catalogue].

Bibliothecæ collegii regalis medicorum Londinensis catalogus (with an Appendix).
London, Royal College of Physicians. 1757.
Octavo, 176 leaves (large paper), foliated as [2] 350, and 174 additional interleaves as blank sheets. 235 x 145 mm. Recent cloth. [21386].
Annotated: various, unattributed.

There was much discussion in the College on producing another catalogue after Salusbury, and several survive in manuscript. Between 1727 and c.1740, Massey compiled a written list, alphabetical by author, of printed books and manuscripts, and with additions in various other hands. The 1757 printed version lists 6650 volumes, fewer than in 1740 (8750) indicating that the disposal of duplicates recommended by Comitia was thorough. The cost of paper and printing for the 1757 catalogue was £48.8s.0d paid to Mr Henry Woodfall of Paternoster Row; £1.11s.6d for correcting the proofs; and £10.10s.0d to Mr E. Noble, a bookseller, for 'making the catalogue'. Massey was given ten guineas for his efforts. A second eighteenth-century catalogue in manuscript, on which the 1757 printed catalogue may originally have been based, remained in use with additions of books and manuscripts up to 1820. Several lists of books bequeathed to the library in the nineteenth century – including those of Thomas Gisborne (d.1806), Matthew Baillie and Arthur Farre (1811–87) – and other acquisitions were prepared. In 1825 a four-volume catalogue, in manuscript, was written. This may be in William Macmichael's (1784–1839) hand. In 1827 appeared John Latham's *Bibliothecæ collegii regalis medicorum Londinensis catalogus. MD CCCXXVII*. This was the first catalogue prepared after the College moved to Pall Mall East. At the end is a list of the manuscripts in the College library (198); and a 'Memorandum of an examination of the Library, made pursuant to the President's directions, in order to ascertain the number of books missing.' A three-volume catalogue was prepared by William Munk in 1856. And in 1861, it was proposed that Mr B. R. Wheatley catalogue books at £1 per hundred. The three volumes were ready by September 1863 at a cost of £126.12s.0d, and were sent for binding with a list of manuscripts. This seems to have gone astray. In 1912, Joseph Payne and Horace Barlow (1884–1954) produced a bound catalogue by alphabetical order, unnumbered but with approximately twenty items on each of the 1354 pages (c. 28,000). A report in 1922 drew attention to the many deficiencies of the archival catalogue and the urgent need to improve access to this valuable resource. The archives were catalogued by Barlow in 1924. A more complete version was produced by William Bishop (1903–61) in 1928 and additions and corrections added in manuscript by Leonard Payne until 1969.

OPPOSITE: Allegorical frontispiece from Edwards' *A natural history of uncommon birds* (1743–51)

WILLIAM HEBERDEN (1710–1801).
[Medical Transactions].

Medical Transactions published by the College of Physicians in London. Volume the first.

London, S. Baker and J. Dodsley. 1768.

Octavo, 243 leaves, paginated as xiv, 472. 305 x 130 mm. Twentieth-century half-calf with cloth boards. [43521].

Inscribed: W[illiam] Russell.

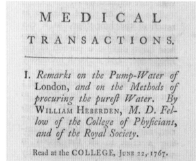

Medical journals were developed in the seventeenth century. Previously, many important items that later appeared in this format were published as individual tracts. Much of interest probably went unpublished. It is estimated that thirty-seven medical journals were founded in Great Britain during the eighteenth century but most did not survive more than a few issues: early publications were *Medicina curiosa: or a variety of new communications in physic, chirurgery, and anatomy* etc. (published by Thomas Basset at The George in Fleet Street on 17 June and 23 October 1684); and *Hippocrates ridens, or joco-serious reflections on the impudence and mischiefs of quacks and illiterate pretenders to physic* (four issues in 1686). In 1766, the College library was given responsibility for producing *Medical Transactions of the Royal College of Physicians in London*. Under the guidance of Heberden, Comitia voted on the suitability for publication of items presented in the Theatre. Sufficient material was available by 1767 to produce a first volume. The twenty-one items include 'Of the night-blindness, or nyctalopia' and 'On the chickenpox' by Heberden; and 'Observations on cancers' by Mark Akenside (1721–70). Other volumes appeared in 1772 and 1785, and six more before publication ceased in 1820 (all also in the College library). A major cost was the production of plates and the binding of volumes, but the *Transactions* were successful and individual volumes often reprinted.

TOP: The first article in *Medical Transactions*, Volume 1 (1768)
ABOVE: William Heberden (1710–1801)

ALBRECHT VON HALLER (1708–77).
[*Bibliotheca medicinæ practicæ*].

Bibliotheca medicinæ practicæ qua scripta ad partem medicinæ practicam facientia a rerum initiis ad A. MDCCLXXV recensentur: Tomus I Ad Annum MDXXXIII; Tomus II Ab Anno 1534 Ad. A. 1647; Tomus III Ab Anno 1648 Ad. A. 1685; Tomus IV Ab Anno 1686 Ad. A. 1707.

Basle and Bern, Joh[annes] Schweighauser and Em[anuel] Haller. 1776–88.

Quarto, 1268 leaves, paginated as viii 540; vi 722; [4] 650; viii 598. 270 x 215 mm, opened but with uncut deckled edges. Later half-roan with cloth boards, now worn. [1596 to 1599].

Inscribed: 4 vols £3. 13. 6.

Annotated: Vol I, with shelf-marks corresponding (presumably) to holdings in the College library.

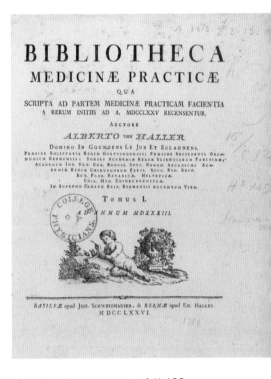

The first bibliographies to include medical works were produced by Marsilio Ficino (1433–99: *De sole et lumine*, 1493, listing his own books and with reference to others); Johann Tritheim (1462–1516), who listed incunabula (*Liber de scriptoribus ecclesiasticis*, 1494); Symphorien Champier (1472–1539: *De medicine claris scriptoribus*, 1506); and Conrad Gesner (1516–65: *Bibliotheca universalis* 1551–58, Appendix, 1555). These efforts were dwarfed by Haller's bibliographies. Haller failed to secure a position as director of the City Hospital in Bern on the grounds that he was a poet not a physician; and he was subsequently also unsuccessful in applying for the professorship of history (on two occasions). Haller was appointed librarian to the city and there he learned skills in bibliography. After producing bibliographies of botany (1771), anatomy (1774) and surgery (1774), Haller published his listing of books on practical medicine, arranged chronologically and with a brief account of each author, a synopsis of 11,400 books and some account of their physical structure but no collation. It is estimated that Haller included 95 per cent of all important published works and wrote informative notes on 20 per cent. He became a recluse in the pursuit of this enterprise reading continuously – before, during and after meals, on horseback, and when walking and writing including transferring to his left hand within twenty-four hours of breaking his right wrist.

WILLIAM HUNTER (1718–83). [The anatomy of the human gravid uterus].

Anatomia uteri humani gravidi tabulis illustrata … The anatomy of the human gravid uterus exhibited in figures by William Hunter physician extraordinary to the Queen, professor of anatomy in the Royal Academy, and Fellow of the Royal and Antiquarian Societies. Printed in Birmingham by John Baskerville, 1774.

London, S. Baker, G. Leigh, T. Cadell, D. Wilson, G. Nicol and J. Murray. 1774.

Broad-sheet, 20 leaves, not paginated, and 34 plates [JV Rymsdyk delin¹; and a large number of different engravers]. 610 x 455 mm. Nineteenth-century half-calf with marbled paper boards. [22140].

Stamped: Sir Arthur Denham.

Inserted: (1) letter from Arthur Denham dated 4 January 1931: Dear Sir, My old and valued friend Dr Dawtrey Drewitt told me this afternoon that you might be glad to receive on behalf of the College of Physicians an atlas folio copy of William Hunter's 'Anatomy of the Human Gravid Uterus' which has a preface by my great-grandfather Thomas Denham MD and which was published in the year of the latter's death, viz 1815. I have two other books, with illustrations, respectively published in 1787 and 1815, but these are large quartos. If the College library does not possess copies of these I shall be pleased to present them, or either of them. Some thirty years ago I offered a work of Peter Shaw MD physician to George III which the College did me the honour to accept. Amongst those with whom I am remotely connected are Mathew Baillie, John and William Hunter, Sir Benjamin Brodie and Sir Richard Croft, and my father Hon George Denham was a Trustee of the Hunterian Museum on the ground of his kinship, so that, since the member of my family for whom I collected these books and many other relics takes not the slightest interest in my hobby, I feel that there could be no better repository than your library. My club, the United University, is almost opposite and if you would let me call and see you one day I might be able to suggest the College's acceptance of other things, Yours very faithfully Arthur Denman; (2) An account of this issue of Dr Hunter's plates on the gravid uterus with the annexed notes taken from another edition dated 1 September 1815 by Thomas Denham; (3) engraving of Thomas Denham, avocat de la reine Caroline, afterwards Lord Chief Justice of England and only son of Dr Thomas Denham, cut through to show script (on verso), avocat de la reine Caroline en 1820; (4) portrait of William Hunter from an original picture by Mason Chamberlain.

Inscribed: (1) Charles Mingay Sydin April 1818. This was bought at the late Sir Richard Croft auction who shot himself on the [13ᵗʰ] day of [February] 1818 in Devonshire Place Marylebone where he was engaged to deliver Mrs T[ownsend]; (2) To George Dickens esqe from his much obliged servant Charles Minghay Sydin; (3) Bought by Arthur Denham 1894, great nephew of the above-mentioned Sir Richard Croft for 18/- at Kimpton's in Holborn. The portraits were inserted by him … and the book was rebound by his librarian.

This is the only medical book published by John Baskerville (1706–75), who took up printing aged fifty, making his own type and having paper woven without chain lines (although this copy is on laid paper). He made his ink from lampblack and used oil that was blacker and dried more rapidly. His wooden presses imposed a shallower impression of the type. The freshly printed sheets were pressed between hot copper to produce a burnished finish. He described his methods in the preface to his second book, John Milton's *Paradise lost* (1758). Baskerville type is modern in the sense that the weight of the strokes varies, and the serifs on terminals of the main strokes are pointed, not clubbed. The type, punched by John Handy (d.1792), is slender, well balanced and aesthetic. The 'Q', with its wide lower serif reaching under the neighbouring 'u' and the 'g', are notable features. At Baskerville's death, the typeface and other printing materials were offered by his wife to Georg Christoph Lichtenberg (1742–99) for £4000 but eventually went to Pierre Beaumarchais (1732–99) in 1779; and from there, via a French foundry, to Cambridge University Press. Unsuccessful as a portrait painter, Jan van Rymsdyk (1730–90) slaved in a freezing Soho garret for the perfectionist Hunter, drawing the putrid abortions and cadavers of destitute women. His original chalk illustrations for the anatomical treatises on the gravid uterus by William Smellie (1697–1763: 1754) and Hunter are now in the University of Glasgow library, to which Hunter left 600 manuscripts, 534 incunabula, twelve Caxtons and 12,000 printed books. Stored at Great Windmill Street for some years after his death, these were handed over to Glasgow by Matthew Baillie in 1807. The collection was accommodated in a special building and relocated to the new museum in 1872.

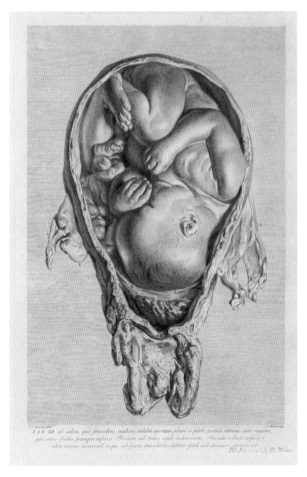

This is the only medical book published by John Baskerville (1706–75), who took up printing aged fifty, making his own type and having paper woven without chain lines.

The child in the womb in its natural situation from Hunter's *The anatomy of the human gravid uterus* TAB XII (1774). The legend shows Baskerville type and the elaborate swash italic capitals P, N, D and H.

GEORGE EDWARDS (1694–1773).
[A natural history of uncommon birds].

(1) A natural history of uncommon birds, and of some other rare and undescribed animals, quadrupedes fishes reptiles insects … exhibited in two hundred and ten copper-plates, from designs copied immediately from nature, and curiously coloured after life. With a full and accurate description of each figure. In four parts … ; (2) A natural history of birds most of which have not been figured or described, and others very little known, from obscure or too brief descriptions without figures, or from figures very ill designed: containing the figures of sixty-one birds and two quadrupeds engrav'd on fifty-three copper plates, af[t]er curious original drawings from life, and exactly colour'd. With full and accurate descriptions. To which is added, an appendix by way of illustration, part II; (3) A natural history of birds, the most of which have not hitherto been figured or described, and the rest, by reason of obscure, or too brief descriptions, without figures, or of figures very ill design'd, are hitherto but little known. This part exhibits the representations of fifty-nine birds, engraven on fifty-two copper plates, and coloured in their natural and proper colours, after curious original paintings, design'd from the life: with a full and accurate description of each bird. Part III; (4) A natural history of birds, the most of which have not hitherto either been figured or described, and the rest, by reason of obscure, or too brief descriptions, without figures, or of figures very ill designed, are hitherto but little known. Containing the representations of thirty-nine birds, engraven on thirty-seven copper plates, after curious original drawings from life; together with a full and accurate description of each. To which are added, by way of Appendix sixteen copper-plates, representing the figures of many curious and undescribed animals such as quadripedes (both land and amphibious), serpents, fishes and insects: the whole containing fifty-three copper-plates, which is the full number given in each of the foregoing parts of this work. Every bird, beast etc. is colour'd from the original painting, according to nature. Part IV.

London, Royal College of Physicians. 1743, 1747, 1750 and 1751.

Folio, 158 leaves, paginated as [4] xx 53 with engraved frontispiece and 52 plates; iv 53–128 [8] 106 (sic)–157 with 52 plates; [8] 158–249 with 53 plates [engraved by Johann Sebastian Leitner (1715–1795)]. 295 x 225 mm. Contemporary morocco with roll-tooled borders incorporating birds and insects, and gilt edges, each volume rebacked. [12781 to 12784].

Edwards was apprenticed to a London merchant but disliked trade and left in 1716 to live in self-confessed idleness, studying natural history and learning to draw and paint. He travelled abroad and made a living out of sketches of animals on his return. Sloane gave him a studio, where Edwards' illustrations, mainly of dead birds obtained abroad, were prepared. He learned etching from Mark Catesby (1683–1749). Although Edwards refused nomination as a fellow, he did receive the Royal Society's Copley Medal in 1750. Edwards was appointed Bedell at the College of Physicians in 1733. In that capacity, he was the second person, after Mr Perkins (n.d.), to take responsibility for the library when the Harveian librarianship lapsed between the tenure of Tyson (in 1750) and the appointment of Munk (in 1857). Several of Edwards' books on natural history were published by the College, for which he was regularly voted fees of five guineas. Edwards resigned as Bedell on 20 June 1760 and was given an additional five guineas in recognition of the gift of his book on birds. In retirement, he published further books on ornithology, including a volume on South American birds purloined from a French ship by Captain Washington Shirley (1722–78), later fifth Earl Ferrers.

OPPOSITE: The red and blue-headed parakeet from Edwards' *A natural history of uncommon birds* (1751) part IV, plate 176

shed according to Act of Parliament December 1745 by George Edwards

176

MICHAEL SERVETUS (c.1511–53).
[Christianismi restitutio].

Christianismi restitvtio. Totius ecclesiæ apostolicæ est ad sua limina vocatio, in integrum restituta cognitione Dei, fidei Christi, iustificationis nostræ, regenerationis baptismi, et cænæ domini manducationis. Restituto denique nobis regno cælesti, Babylonis impiæ captiuitate soluta, et Antichristo cum suis penitus destructo … [Script in Hebrew and Greek, 'And at that time shall Michael stand up. And war broke out in heaven'] MDLIII.

Nuremberg, C.G. von Murr. 1790.

Octavo, 368 leaves, paginated as 734 [2]. 190 x 115 mm. Nineteenth-century vellum, marbled edges. [11817].

Bookplate: (1) C Inglis MD.

Inserted: (1) Bought of Nat. Smith Surgeon London 2 Oct 1722 2s 5d (relating to another book); (2) many images and cuttings from catalogues and newspapers some relating to Calvin and Servetus including notice of a copy of Servetus' De trinitate divina (1723) £1 12s 0d, and Syruporum universa ratio (1537) 'so rare that Mosheim, the biographer of Servetus, was unable to procure a copy'; (3) text on Servetus from another publication: Michael Servetus, like another Simon Magus, having conversed long among the Mahometans and the Jewes, and being excellently well furnished with their imaginous opinions begat, both out of Divinity, and the general treasury of Christian Religion, a monstrous issue of opinions. … in the year one thousand five hundred fifty and three he was (how great is the obstinacy of blasphemy) being at that time ecstatically hardened and intoxicated, consecrated to the avenging flames; (4) Infelix eruditio est scire quod multi nascient etiam periculosa scire quod omnes ignorant – Gaulmin; (5) Oratio anniversaria habita in amphitheatre Collegii Regalis Medicorum … from a volume 'Orationes anniversaria belonging to the R' Medical Society …; (6) In laudem clarissimi doctrissimi et magni viri Thomæ Pelletii præsidis Collegii Regalis Medicorum et tunc in terres ornamentum erat sicut Hesperus et pleides hodie inter lumina coeli coruscunt et qui primus inter homines e tenebris sanguinis motu carmine illustravit (printed in black letter on thin paper; (7) this book contains the first statement as to the blood passing from the right to the left side of the heart through the lungs see p 170.

Michael Servetus first came into conflict with theologians through the publication of *De trinitatis erroribus* (1531) in Lyons where, working in the printing trade as a corrector in the press of Melchior (c. 1490–c. 1570) and Gaspard Trechsel (n.d.), his dogmatic views on the Trinity excited criticism. *Christianismi restitutio* was circulated in manuscript and published in 1553 by Balthasar Arnollet (n.d.) of Vienne (France) – place and printer chosen for their obscurity. The book describes the pulmonary circulation and has much to say on the physiology of the brain. But Servetus could not resist trying to put right the opinions of John Calvin (1509–64). The text was deemed to promote anabaptism and anti-trinitaranism and, on 27 October 1553, Servetus was burned at the stake for heresy along with most copies of his book. Calvin had proposed that the sentence be commuted to beheading but 'when Servetus was carried to the place of execution, Calvin stood at a window and smiled when he saw him go by … and was far from being much displeased at the spectacle'. Only three of 1000 copies of *Christianismi restitutio* survive: one in Edinburgh, which lacks the title page and first sixteen leaves; one in the Bibliothèque Nationale (previously owned by Richard Mead); and one in Vienna. A reprint was planned in 1723 but this was abandoned after 250 pages were printed. Those copies were also seized and burned by the Bishop of London, on 29 May 1723. Five copies survive, one owned by the Medical Society of London. Eventually the further reprint from Nuremberg (1790) brought details of the book to a wider readership, but this also is rare.

Ad quam rem eſt prius intelligenda ſubſtantialis generatio ipſius vitalis ſpiritus, qui ex aëre inſpirato, et ſubtiliſſimo ſanguine componitur, et nutritur. Vitalis ſpiritus in ſiniſtro cordis ventriculo ſuam originem habet, iuuantibus maxime pulmonibus ad ipſius generationem. Eſt ſpiritus tenuis, caloris vi elaboratus, flauo colore, ignea potentia, vt ſit quaſi ex puriori ſanguine lucidus vapor, ſubſtantiam in ſe continens aquæ, aëris, et ignis. Generatur ex facta in pulmonibus mixtione inſpirati aëris cum elaborato ſubtili ſanguine, quem dexter ventriculus cordis ſiniſtro communicat. Fit autem communicatio hæc non per parietem cordis medium, vt vulgo creditur, ſed magno artificio a dextro cordis ventriculo, longo per pulmones ductu, agitatur ſanguis ſubtilis: a pulmonibus præparatur, flauus efficitur: et a vena arterioſa, in arteriam venoſam transfunditur. Deinde in ipſa arteria venoſa inſpirato aëri miſcetur, exſpiratione a fuligine repurgatur. Atque ita tandem a ſiniſtro cordis ventriculo totum mixtum per diaſtolem attrahitur, apta ſupellex, vt fiat ſpiritus vitalis.

ABOVE: Description of the pulmonary circulation in 1553 at page 170, seventy-five years before Harvey
LEFT: Michael Servetus (c. 1511–53) pasted into this copy of Servetus' *Christianismi restitutio* (1790)

The text was deemed to promote anabaptism and anti-trinitaranism and, on 27 October 1553, Servetus was burned at the stake for heresy along with most copies of his book.

EDWARD JENNER (1749–1823).
[Regulations and transactions].

Regulations and transactions of the Gloucestershire Medical Society instituted May 1788.

Folio, 69 leaves, some original pagination, foliated later in manuscript as 59 [some not marked and others containing folded, or more than one document]. 320 x 200 mm. Half-vellum with marbled boards (dated 8/1/82). [MS736].

Manuscript [sheets, letters and fragments in various hands including Edward Jenner (leaves 11 and 12, dated July 30 1788; and undated), John Heathfield Hickes, Thomas Paytherus, Daniel Ludlow and Caleb Hillier Parry]. c.1788.

Inserted: (1) Book-label: No 1267 From the library of Sir William Osler, Bart. Oxford (received on 4 Oct 1928); (2) copy of note and catalogue entry overleaf WWF [William Francis]; (3) leaves i and ii are typescripts of the entry in *Bibliotheca Osleriana*, in press 1928 pp 127–8.

Inscribed: See note in this of Jenner's paper on hydatids of kidney & BMJ 1896. 1 [p 1296] for reprint of one of these papers; WO.

[*With*] [Edward Jenner] Diary, containing his observations on the natural history of the cuckoo, and notes on his dissections of other birds and of various domestic animals. [April 26th 1787– April 29th 1806]. c. 1806.

Manuscript. Quarto, 79 leaves, paginated as [39] 25–100 [43] (of which the index and entry for 15 January 1787 have inverted text). 205 x 160 mm. Quarter-morocco and vellum corners over original marbled paper boards. [MS372].

Bookplate: (Rev) George Charles Jenner (1767–1846: Edward Jenner's nephew).

Inserted: cutting from Sotheby's catalogue, lot 483 relating to a letter from Jenner to Doctor Hickes on researches into the behaviour of the cuckoo, sold 22 January 1958.

Inscribed: George Charles Jenner Woodford near Berkeley Gloucestershire.

ABOVE: Signatures of members of the Gloucestershire Medical Society (1788)

Jenner had heard from a countrywoman that, having already had cowpox, she would not catch smallpox.

Jenner had heard from a countrywoman that, having already had cowpox, she would not catch smallpox. His work was first published as *An inquiry into the cause and effects of the variolae vaccinae, a disease discovered in some of the western counties of England, particularly Gloucestershire, and known by the name of the cow-pox* (1798). Members of the Gloucestershire Medical Society, which met at the Fleece Inn, Rodborough, were Caleb Hillier Parry (1755–1822), John Heathfield Hickes (1751–1808), Thomas Paytherus (1752–1828), Daniel Ludlow (n.d.) and Jenner. On 28 July 1790, Hickes read a paper on 'Observations & Experiments made upon persons labouring under an eruptive fever which appeared in several parts of Glos'tershire in the latter end of 1789'; and, in September 1790, he wrote a fourteen-page manuscript present in the volume (eventually dated 1792), to which he and Jenner added further particulars relating to swinepox. Hickes advocated inoculating individuals who had already experienced swinepox with smallpox, and details of five cases are included. There is mention of this procedure being carried out on Jenner's son Edward. William Osler bought books from an early age and was acquisitive yet generous in giving to medical libraries. Although most of his books (the 7783 entries in *Bibliotheca Osleriana; a catalogue of books illustrating the history of medicine and science, collected, arranged and annotated by Sir William Osler, and*

bequeathed to McGill University, 1929) formed the Osler library at McGill, he gave the College of Physicians the *Regulations and transactions* etc. and four other books. The diary had probably been presented by Geoffrey Marston on 2 February 1888. Here, Jenner points out that there is, transiently, a depression in the back of a recently hatched cuckoo which allows it to expel other eggs from the nest it has occupied, work for which he was elected to fellowship of the Royal Society.

No. 1267

FROM

THE LIBRARY

OF

SIR WILLIAM OSLER, BART.

OXFORD

ABOVE: Ownership label of Sir William Osler (1849–1919)

MATTHEW BAILLIE (1761–1823).
[Morbid anatomy]

The morbid anatomy of some of the most important parts of the human body.

London, J. Johnston and G. Nicol. 1793.

Octavo, two volumes, 101 and 74 leaves, paginated as [8] xxviii 166; [167] -314, each volume interleaved, with 83 and 77 sheets. 200 x 125 mm. Twentieth-century half-morocco with marbled paper boards. [MS101 and MS102].

Inscribed: M Baillie, in each volume.

Annotated: interleaved sheets with changes and proposed textual deletions in manuscript, some stylistic and some factual, in the author's hand, in each volume.

[With] Matthew Baillie. A series of engravings, accompanied with explanations, which are intended to illustrate the morbid anatomy of some of the most important parts of the human body.

London, J. Johnston and G. Nicol. 1799.

Quarto, 115 leaves, paginated as [2] ii 3–228, in 10 fascicules with 203 figures on 73 plates. 325 x 250 mm. Nineteenth-century morocco with gilt tooling, rebacked. [19678].

Inscribed: M Baillie.

[With] William Clift. Twenty-four proofs and draft versions of engravings relating to Fascicules 2 (plate 1), 3 (1), 7 (3), 8 (8), 9 (4 and 8) and 10 (3 and 8) marked William Cliff delineavit or Willm Clift del^t or variations thereof. c1793.

Folio, 27 sheets. c. 320 x 230 mm. Half-morocco with preserved earlier marbled paper boards. [MS103].

Inserted: Label for Staunton & Son, Stationers, Strand, London removed to No 1. Craven Street.

Annotated: (1) Fascicule 9 (4) Published by Dr Baillie April 20 1802 … to be inverted in each plate and sent to him immediately; (2) Fascicule 10 (8), an image of cerebral haemorrhage (Figs 1 and 2) with indications for points of interest and (Fig 2) to be engraved with the lower end upwards, so that the whole will be inverted.

Matthew Baillie, last owner of the gold-headed cane, was a significant donor to the College library. As nephew of John (1728–93) and William Hunter, with whom he lived after moving to London from Glasgow, Baillie helped to prepare specimens and used their collections during his vacations from Balliol College, Oxford. He inherited the Great Windmill Street School on William Hunter's death. Baillie was instrumental in founding the Medical and Chirurgical Society in 1806. This merged with eighteen specialist societies to become the Royal Society of Medicine in 1907. Baillie presented the first fascicule of the atlas to the College library on 23 December 1793, and fascicules 3–6 and 8–10 between 7 April 1800 and 22 December 1802. He annotated the text in preparation for the second edition of the *Morbid anatomy*. For example, at page 312, the text reads: 'That particular substance called the glandula pituitaria is liable to very few diseases'. This is deleted with the comment: 'I have never seen it in any decided or obvious alteration from its natural structure. It is somewhat firmer in one person than another, but this never struck me to be disease.' The second edition (page 451) reads:

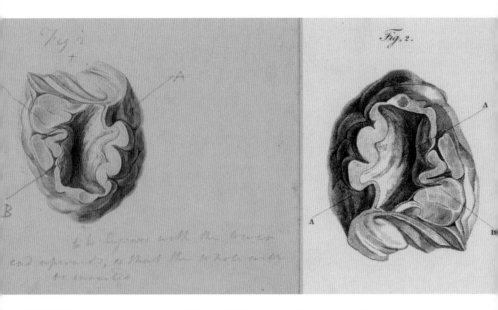

ABOVE: Original watercolour showing a fluid-filled cavity following cerebral haemorrhage with instructions to the printer and the engraved image as published in Baillie's *Morbid anatomy* etc. (1799)

This gland is very little liable to be affected by disease. It has only occurred to me to observe in it one morbid change. It was, in that case, enlarged to twice its natural size, and was converted into a substance, possessing an obscurely fibrous structure.

The advertisement in the first fasciculus of Baillie's atlas indicates that 'the drawings will be made by a young man, who is not only very well skilled in his own arts, but who possesses a considerable share of knowledge in anatomy'. Spotted as artistically talented by John Hunter's wife, William Clift (1775–1849) was apprenticed as anatomical assistant to the surgeon, carrying out dissections and writing accounts to dictation. After Hunter's death, Clift curated the collection from 1793 to 1843, and he saved a number of items that might otherwise have been lost when (Sir) Everard Home (1756–1832) purged his late brother-in-law's manuscripts in 1823. Clift's retainer as conservator and protector of the Hunterian collection, acquired by the Government and donated to the Company of Surgeons, was £80 per annum with use of a house in Castle Street (and an allowance for coal).

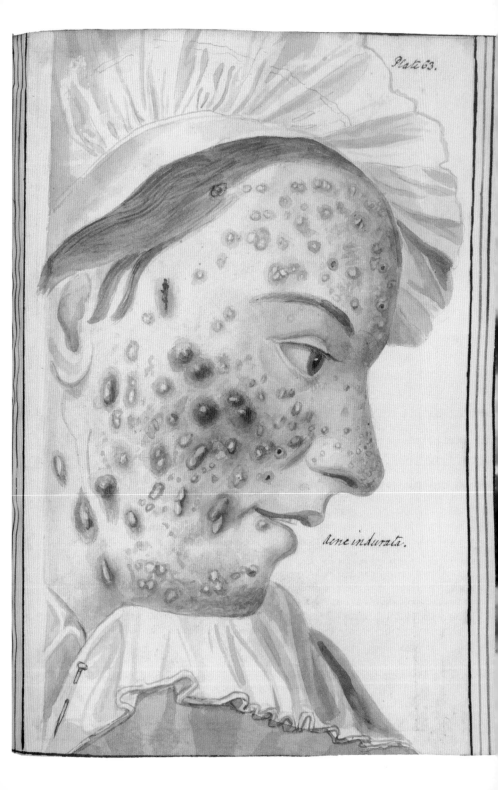

Plate 63.

acne indurata.

NINETEENTH CENTURY

ROBERT WILLAN (1757–1812).
[On cutaneous diseases].

On cutaneous diseases. Vol. 1. Containing Ord. 1. Papulae. Ord. II. Squamae. Ord. III. Exanthemata. Ord. IV. Bullæ.

London, J. Johnson. 1808.

Quarto, 282 leaves, paginated as [2] xvi 17-110 [2] 111–556 [4] with colour-printed and hand-finished plates I– XXXIII [published between October 1st 1796 and January 1st 1808: Syd[ney] Edwards, W Darton, J Walker, Strutt delin'; Perry, J Strutt, Sailliar sculp'] . 260 x 215 mm. Twentieth-century quarter morocco and marbled paper boards. [19324].

Annotated: occasional marginal markings.

[*With*] **Thomas Bateman (1778–1821). [Delineations of cutaneous diseases]**

Delineations of cutaneous diseases: exhibiting the characteristic appearances of the principal genera and species comprised in the classification of the late Dr Willan; and completing the series of engravings begun by that author.

London, Longman, Longman, Hurst, Rees, Orme and Brown. 1817.

Quarto, 77 leaves, paginated as viii ii [144], with 72 colour-printed and hand-finished plates and text on separate pages [dated from July 1st 1815 to Oct' 1st 1817 drawn by TB (Thomas Bateman) and others]. 265 x 205 mm. Later half-calf with marbled paper boards, rebacked. [19321].

Inscribed: M Baillie on title page.

[With] [Thomas Bateman] Delineations of cutaneous diseases. No date.

Manuscript. Quarto, 144 leaves, 72 coloured drawings and engravings each with accompanying text [some marked Syd(ney) Edwards Delin'; most are original watercolours with manuscript titles, unsigned]. 225 x 180 mm. Twentieth-century half-morocco with cloth boards. [MS158].

Inserted: leaf from Sotheby's catalogue 8 June 1906 with item 1026 marked Bateman (Thos. MD) *Delineations of cutaneous diseases*. Original manuscript in the author's handwriting with coloured drawings and engravings, half-bound no date.

[*With*] **[Thomas Bateman] [Illustrations of skin diseases]. No date.**

A collection of 79 watercolours corresponding to published plates, with others appearing in *Delineations of cutaneous diseases* etc.

Large folio. 49 leaves, foliated as [48] [1]. 535 x 385 mm. Full morocco. [MS159].

Annotated: author's naming of each condition and with instructions to the printer; some signed F. Perry del; T.B. delin; Syd Edwards del.; G. Boyne; W.T. Strutt del.; Cruikshank del 25 Dec 1806; W. Darton.

[*With*] **[Thomas Bateman]. [Illustrations of skin diseases]. c. 1792–1814.**

A collection of 97 images, mostly watercolours, in various sizes, some double-sided by Bateman or various artists [most undated and unsigned]. Disbound and contained in a loose-leaf folder. [MS748].

Willan and Bateman founded modern dermatology. The library has 176 watercolours completed between 1792 and 1814 drawn and painted by Bateman or various other artists. Some are annotated with instructions to the engraver. Many appear in the printed edition of *Delineations of cutaneous diseases* 1817; others are unpublished. Bateman added clinical details and dates (e.g. *Pompholyx suitinus* Epsom, 15 July 1813) and named his patients (e.g. Mrs Alry, No 6, Middle Road, Holborn; and Mrs

H, Islington, July 1814, diagnosed with *Rupia prominens*). The College acquired
the manuscript of Bateman's book at auction from Sotheby's in 1906. The original
watercolours were given by Mr Ramsay of Cheltenham in 1862. The College bought
a copy of Willan's *On cutaneous diseases* for 15s on 25 March 1799. It transpires
that this had been issued in parts and the purchase was of Part 1, issued in 1799.
Parts 2 and 3 were published in 1801 and 1804 and the whole, revised, with Part
4 and the title page, *On cutaneous diseases*, in 1808. On the basis that a German
translation exists, published in 1799–1806, it is thought that an even earlier English
version of the work, now lost, must have been published. On Willan's death in 1812
his illustrations became the property of Bateman, who added to the work, publishing
Delineations of cutaneous diseases in 1817. Of the seventy-two illustrations published
by Bateman, six are borrowed from Willan's original series.

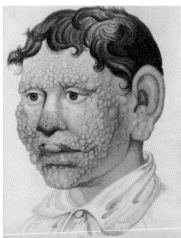

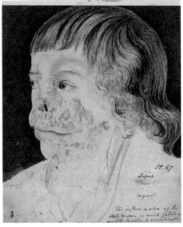

**Willan and Bateman
founded modern
dermatology.
The library has
176 watercolours
completed between
1792 and 1814 drawn
and painted by
Bateman or various
other artists.**

ABOVE AND PAGE 86: Original watercolours and published plates: page 86 and clockwise above
Bateman original for plate 63, acne indurata; Bateman (1817) plate 68, elephantiasis; Willan (1808) plate
21, rubiola; and Bateman original for plate 67, lupus

CHARLES BELL (1774–1842).
[Idea of a new anatomy of the brain].

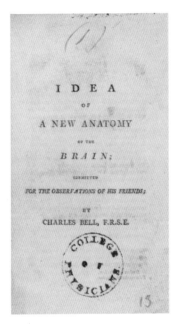

Idea of a new anatomy of the brain: submitted for the observation of his friends, by Charles Bell FRSE.

Privately published; printed by Strahan and Preston, Printers-Street, London. 1811.

Octavo, 18 leaves, paginated as 36. 170 x 105 mm. With four other contemporary items, rebound in twentieth-century buckram. [22875].

Inscribed: (1) Contents. 1: Bell (Cha) Idea of a new Anat of the Brain. 2: Stanger (C) Remarks on the necessity and means of suppressing contagious fever in the Metropolis. 1804. 3: Creaser (Thomas) Evidences of the utility of vaccine inoculation. 1801. 4: Waterworth (T.L.) On the nature and properties of the aluminous chalybeate water at Sand Rocks in the Isle of Wight. 1814. 5: Ware (James) A letter to the members of the Society for relieving the widows and orphans of medical men. 1810; (2) 24 Soho Square, in contemporary hand [probably James Newman (1790–1830), supplier of artists' materials].

The rarest of all Charles Bell's works, *Idea of a new anatomy,* etc., addresses the theory of reflexes. It was prepared for private distribution to his friends but became the evidence on which a celebrated spat relating to the 'the way in and the way out' of the spinal cord turned. Bell stimulated the posterior and anterior spinal roots and, correctly, observed responses consistent with sensory and motor functions, respectively. But because he was motivated by understanding the roles of the cerebrum and cerebellum on spinal anatomy and function, his interpretation of the experiments went awry. He concluded that the anterior root responds to the cerebrum, and transmits both motor and sensory functions; whereas the posterior root is connected to the cerebellum and subserves visceral activities. François Magendie (1783–1855) got it right, as Bell then saw, but he argued that Magendie, who had read the *Idea of a new anatomy of the brain*, could not have done his work without knowledge of Bell's experimental method of selective nerve root stimulation. Rather than acknowledge this improvement on his own ideas, Bell subsequently published papers in *Philosophical Transactions* and a monograph (*An exposition of the natural system of the nerves of the human body*, 1824) that subtly altered his position and claimed priority, offering himself as 'the Harvey of the nervous system'. Meanwhile Magendie allowed it to be known that he had received Bell's papers after his own publication and congratulated 'Mr Bell on so nearly discovering the function of the spinal roots'. This tangled version of events was completed by Alexander Walker (1779–1852), who argued that the anterior roots are sensory and the posterior motor (*Archives of Universal Science,* 1809), always maintaining that this was correct, and claiming priority over both Bell and Magendie whose efforts had merely 'borrowed, inverted, and blundered about' work that had occupied Walker since his youth.

AUGUSTUS D'ESTE (1794–1848).
[The case of Augustus d'Este].

The case of Augustus d'Este.

Quarto, 41 leaves, paginated as [4] 78. 200 x 155 mm. Contemporary quarter roan with marbled paper boards. [MS125].

Manuscript [in various hands]. December 1822–7 December 1846.

Inserted: (1) entry for January 1844; (2) copy of the soothing prescription; (3) copy of letter from Rev B.G. Bartlett to Dr C. E. Newman dated 5 May 1966 confirming that the diary is on permanent loan to the Royal College of Physicians.

Inscribed: (1) (by Augustus d'Este) meaning of description hieroglyphics. M – this mark means Minims. 3 – this mark means Drachm; (2) acquired c. 1941.

[*With*] **Simpson's Gentleman's Almanack and Pocket Journal for the year of our Lord 1847 [Almanac of Augustus d'Este. July 28th 1846 – February 1848].**

London R & A Suttaby, and Peacock and Mansfield. 1847.

Manuscript. Octavo, 109 leaves, paginated as [6] 208 [4]. 165 x 105 mm. Contemporary morocco with gilt-tooling on covers and spine. [MS124].

Inserted: (1) two larger folded sheets with annotations marked 'Continuation of my case working copy, February 1846'; (2) three slips of paper noting accounts.

Annotated: (1) acquired c1941; (2) extensively by Augustus d'Este, and various amanuenses.

This is the earliest personal account of multiple sclerosis. What remained of the diary after pilfering and the attentions of rats was rescued by Douglas Firth (1880–1948) during the Second World War. d'Este was the product of a liaison between Lady Augusta Murray (1768–1830) and Prince Augustus Frederick (1773–1843), Duke of Sussex (sixth son of George III and uncle of Queen Victoria). The King caused the marriage (hurriedly arranged in Rome) to be annulled, thus making the issue illegitimate. Brought up by his mother, the young d'Este behaved, during adolescence and as a young man, in a manner that gave the English aristocracy of the time a deservedly bad name. In 1822, he developed bilateral optic neuritis (he may have had neuromyelitis optica rather than multiple sclerosis) while visiting Scotland. Further episodes occurred and, in 1830, d'Este discovered that he was impotent while attempting a 'professional encounter' on a visit to the seaside resort of Ramsgate in southern England (where eventually he died). By 1843, his walking lacked balance and his symptoms were progressing. He tried many means of preserving his mobility, but all was in vain and d'Este died aged fifty-four having had demyelinating disease for twenty-six years.

ABOVE: Entries for December 1847 documenting the pitiful state of d'Este's impaired walking

WILLIAM MACMICHAEL (1784–1839).
The gold-headed cane.

The gold-headed cane.

London, John Murray. 1827.

Octavo, 181 leaves, paginated as [8] 180, and 87 interleaved sheets. 210 x 130 mm. Nineteenth-century calf with gilt-tooling, in a protective case. [MS113].

Bookplate: Richard Lane Freer.

Inserted: (1) original watercolour of Sir Hans Sloane (bound-in); (2) design for a memorial plaque to Harvey by Richard Mead with inscription in manuscript (bound-in); (3) notice of Harveian oration; (4) advertisement for publication of a facsimile edition on the occasion of the four hundred and fiftieth anniversary of the College (1968) with an introduction by Sir Max (Lord) Rosenheim (1908–72) and notes by Macmichael's great-grandson, Dr Thomas Hunt (1901-80: who donated the book to the College on 12 June 1974), including previously unpublished letters; (5) typescript of two letters relating to restoration from Dr Hunt to Mr L.M. Payne (19 February and 10 September 1963).

Annotated: extensively by Macmichael (and others) mainly on the interleaves.

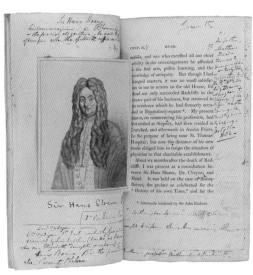

ABOVE: Entry for Sir Hans Sloane annotated for a second edition from Macmichael's *The gold-headed cane* (1847)

Macmichael relates, using a somewhat precious literary device, the imaginary adventures of the cane over a period of nearly 150 years, providing details of conversations and consultations that it overheard, which paint a picture of medical life in the eighteenth and early nineteenth centuries. Eventually, the cane laments its fate. Having previously been carried about by eminent physicians, it is now to be deposited in a corner closet of the library surrounded by the musty manuscripts of defunct doctors. The actual cane was given to the College by the widow of Matthew Baillie, its last owner, when the building at Pall Mall East opened in 1825. *The gold-headed cane* celebrates the principle that the right to practise physic depends on the ethical behaviour of licentiates benefiting from a liberal education and training in classics and the arts. Macmichael focuses on the art of medicine as practised by five royal physicians. The cane belonged to John Radcliffe (1650–1714) and was handed down to Richard Mead, Anthony Askew, William Pitcairn (1712–91) and Matthew Baillie. Pitcairn became President of the College of Physicians of London. Macmichael began his association with the College as Censor and Registrar (1824–29), supervising the move to Pall Mall East in 1825. He also wrote biographies of Linacre, Caius, Harvey, Browne, (Thomas) Sydenham (1624–89), Radcliffe and Baillie in *Lives of British physicians* (1827) published anonymously with eleven other biographies by three different authors.

SAMUEL JOHNSON 1709–84. [Sermons].

Sermons by Samuel Johnson left for publication by John Taylor LI D Prebendary of Westminster. Ripon, T. Procter. 1835.

Octavo, 196 leaves, paginated as [4] 388. 210 x 135 mm. Contemporary morocco with gilt-tooling, inner joints cracked and boards loose; gilt edges over fore-edge painting of Dr Johnson's house, Lichfield. [11861].

Inserted: (1) on card, Samuel Johnson. Sermons. Ripon 1835. With a fore-edge painting of Dr Johnson's House at Lichfield; ladies night 27.4.61. p47. (0) 255; (2) Binders ticket of Procter & Vickers, Ripon.

Fore-edge painting is an English invention dignified by Bernard Middleton as the first completely frivolous binding practice. Partially concealed during routine handling, the painting is viewed by gently splaying the horizontally held fore-edge leaves of the book. During painting, the edges of the leaves are scraped, the paper sized, the paint neither wet nor dry, and the colours generally over-bright. Most fore-edge paintings are on the upper side enabling the artist to brush down the slightly overlapping leaves. A cartoon of the definitive version is sometimes seen on the lower edge but entirely different double fore-edge paintings are also occasionally present. When finished, the flattened leaves are gilded. This fore-edge painting of Samuel Johnson's house in Lichfield depicts a townscape with three houses in profile and a Hansom cab in front, a street with traders and awnings in perspective to the right, two central monuments and several other figures.

ABOVE: Fore-edge painting of Dr Johnson's house in Lichfield from Johnson's *Sermons* (1835). Text and image from Alastair Compston in Davenport *et al.* (2001)

RICHARD BRIGHT (1789–1858).
[Reports of medical cases].

Reports of medical cases, selected with a view of illustrating the symptoms and cure of diseases by a reference to morbid anatomy: Volume II Diseases of the brain and nervous system Part I including inflammation of the brain and its membranes;- acute hydrocephalus;- delirium tremens;- apoplexy;- paraplegia;- concussion;- chronic hydrocephalus;- spina bifida. Volume II Diseases of the brain and nervous system Part II including hysteria;- chorea;- palsy from mercury;- neuralgia;- epilepsy;- tetanus;- and hydrophobia together with a concise statement of the diseased appearances of the brain and its membranes.

London, Longman, Rees, Orme, Brown and Green. 1827–31.

Quarto, two volumes in three, 564 leaves, paginated as xvi 232 [30] with 16 hand-coloured plates; xl [2] 450; [4] (451)–724 [80] with 40 hand-coloured plates. 300 x 240 mm. Contemporary half-morocco, boards detached (Volume 1 rebound to match). [19776 to 19778].

Annotations: occasional, unattributed but later.

[With] [Frederick Say (c.1827–c. 60)]. Original watercolours. c.1825–28

Comprising twenty-one figures for Volume I, and seventeen figures for Volume II on the brain and nervous system; with manuscript note on each verso relating to plate numbers in the printed volumes, mounted on grey card, most signed F. R. Say 1825–28; the corresponding printed plates are signed F.R. Say and identify the engraver as W. Say, 9 Mortimer St. and, later, of 20 Blenheim St. (London); some in Volume II ii are drawn by C. J. Canton, T. & W. Fairland, and Scharfe, and these are engraved by C. T. Fry, C. Hullmandel, and Engelmann and Co. The archive contains additional drawings and watercolours, some with case-notes by Bright, loose and in two small booklets, and case-notes that do not match any illustrations appearing in Reports of medical cases etc., or that post-date publication. [MS159].

Starting with Matthew Baillie, atlases of pathological anatomy with specimens painted by medical illustrators and reproduced as engravings or chromolithographs appeared in the early nineteenth century. In the United Kingdom, the most lavish were those of Robert Carswell (1793–1857:

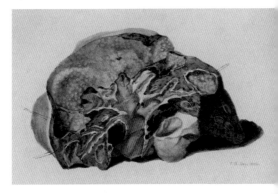

ABOVE: Original watercolour from Bright's *Reports of medical cases* (1827), corresponding to plate X, volume I, case LII, Edward Phalin

Pathological anatomy. Illustrations of the elementary forms of disease, 1838) and James Hope (1801–41: *Principles and illustrations of morbid anatomy*, 1834). In continental Europe, the greatest work was produced by Jean Cruveilhier (1791–1874: *Anatomie pathologique du corps humain* etc., 1829–42). Bright devotes more text to the description of cases than his contemporaries and since Volume II, which is in two parts and constitutes the bulk of his text, concerns only the brain and its appendages, his is the definitive atlas of neuropathology from this period. It outclasses that of Robert Hooper (1773–1835: *The morbid anatomy of the human brain illustrated by coloured engravings of the most frequent and important organic diseases to which that viscus is subject*, 1826). The watercolours and case notes were given to the College by Bright's son, George Charles Bright (1840–1922) on 26 July 1889. It is thought that those unsigned are by Richard Bright himself.

RUDOLF VIRCHOW (1821–1902).
[Cellular pathology].

Die cellularpathologie in ihrer Begründung auf physiologische und pathologische Gewebelehre. Zwanzig vorlesungen gehalten während der Monate Februar, März und April 1858 im pathologischen Institute zu Berlin.

Berlin, August Hirschwald. 1858.

Octavo, 228 leaves, paginated as xvi 440, with 144 figures in the text. 215 x 135 mm. Half-calf with marbled paper boards. [25129].

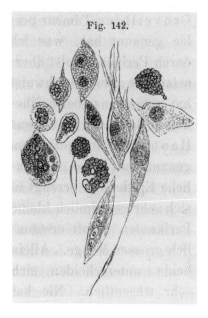

Fig. 142.

ABOVE: Cancer cells from Virchow's *Cellular pathology* (1858) Fig 142, page 429

Virchow abandoned his initial interest in theology to study medicine, eventually establishing an Institute of Pathology at the Charité Hospital in Berlin. In 1847 Virchow founded *Archiv für pathologische Anatomie und Physiologie und für klinische Medizin*, which prioritised papers forming the basis for histopathology. Modern cell and molecular biology derive from his concept of the cell as the unit of health and disease. This builds on the work of Theodor Schwann (1810–82) and Robert Remak (1815–65): 'all cells (come) from cells'. Virchow introduced a systematic approach to autopsy, described and named many conditions, and proposed their pathological mechanisms. For a scientist and progressive parliamentarian, Virchow was curiously stubborn about evolution, referring to Charles Darwin (1809–82) as an 'ignoramus' and his own student Ernst Haeckel (1834–1919) as a 'fool'. Virchow published the twenty lectures on cellular pathology delivered to practising physicians in Berlin during February, March and April 1858 in support of his theory of life out of which the science of pathology was henceforth constructed. The lectures were taken down in stenography by Herr Langenhaum (n.d.) and minimally revised, with woodcuts taken from drawings on the blackboard and microscopic preparations distributed at the time. In offering reformative ideas, Virchow hoped to respect but not be shackled by history, preserving the old and adding the new. An English translation (1860) by Frank Chance (1826–97), licentiate of the Royal College of Physicians, contained amendments made with Virchow's approval, elaborated in a series of fifty letters that they exchanged. Chance had attended the lectures given in March and April 1858.

WILLIAM MUNK (1816–98). [Munk's Roll].

The Roll of the Royal College of Physicians of London; compiled from the annals of the College and from other authentic sources … Vol I 1518 to 1700; Vol II 1701–1800.

London, Longman, Green, Longman and Roberts. 1861.

Octavo, 487 and 441 leaves, paginated as xvi, 472; ix 429; each volume interleaved (243 and 222, respectively). 210 x 135 mm. Contemporary half-morocco with marbled paper boards, hinges loose. [MS2259].

Inserted: letter from H. Morley Fletcher: Burton Corner Petworth Sussex Petworth 17 Nov 30 [19]37, My dear Chaplin, I am leaving for you at the College the original Munk's Roll to be added to the library. The volumes were given to me by Lady Moore after the death of Sir Norman Moore, yrs ever, H Morley Fletcher.

Inscribed: Norman Moore 1911.

Annotated: Extensive corrections and additions on the interleaves and text by Munk throughout, with additional manuscript notes loosely inserted.

The Roll of the Royal College of Physicians of London, commonly known as *Munk's Roll*, provides biographical entries for physicians who were fellows, candidates or licentiates of the College. Later, selection was confined to eminent physicians whose names are recorded in the annals from foundation of the College in 1518 to its move in 1825 from Warwick Lane to Pall Mall East. From Volume IV, the work became *Lives of the fellows of the Royal College of Physicians of London.* The *Roll* was published in eleven volumes to 2004 (switching from chronological to alphabetical listing from Volume VI), and is now available only in electronic format. The first volume of *Munk's Roll*, 'undertaken with the hope of supplying a want I had myself experienced', was ready by April 1855; a second volume was completed by December of that year and a third in June 1856. Each manuscript volume was deposited in the library for the use of fellows. A printed version of Volumes I (1518–1700) and II (1700–1800) followed in 1861, in an edition of 1000 copies at a cost to the College of £194.7s.6d; and Volume III appeared in 1878. In his will, Munk offered the College the interleaved and extensively annotated copy of the second edition of the *Roll* for £500. This was considered too much and nothing was done. In the event, an interleaved copy of the first edition with additions in preparation for the second was bought by Norman Moore, given by Lady Moore to (Herbert) Morley Fletcher (1864–1950), and donated to the College in 1937. The College does also have the interleaved copy of the second, originally offered by Munk, but its provenance is unknown. That volume is itself extensively annotated by Munk and others for preparation of later editions with many typescripts and cuttings pasted in, including extracts from booksellers' and auctioneers' catalogues relating to individual entries (some as late as 1958).

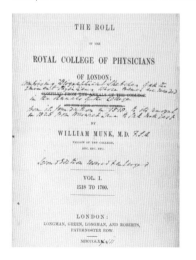

ABOVE: The title page from *Munk's Roll* (1861) annotated for a second edition

ANDREAS VESALIUS
(1514–64). [Tabulæ anatomicæ sex].

Andre Vesalii Tabulæ anatomicæ sex. Six anatomical tables of Andrew Vesalius. Venetiis. Imprimebat B. Vitalis, venetus, sumptibus Ioannis Stephani Calcarensis MDXXXVIII. London: privately printed for Sir William Stirling-Maxwell. MDCCCLXXIV.

London, William Stirling-Maxwell. 1874.

Elephant folio, 12 leaves including engraved title page, text and plates I–VI (all printing on the *recto* only), foliated as 6 [7–12]. 660 x 500 mm. Original quarter morocco with marbled paper boards. [22155].

Although critical of this in others, Vesalius was not above reaching conclusions relating to human structure and function through studying the ape rather than man.

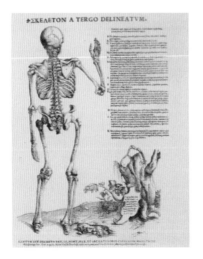

ABOVE: Tabula VI the human skeleton
OPPOSITE: Engraved title page. Both from Vesalius' *Tabulæ anatomicæ sex* (1874)

Towards the end of the Middle Ages, the Church relaxed its prohibition on the dissection of human bodies, and post-mortem examination was introduced in the fourteenth century, after the Black Death. But the teaching of anatomy based on dissection had to wait another 200 years for approval. In 1538, Vesalius published *Tabulæ anatomicæ sex* comprising six anatomical plates based on dissections. Vesalius tells us that he drew the first three, and the other plates are the work of Jan van Calcar (c.1499–1546). A seventh plate on the nerves, promised by Vesalius for the *Tabulæ*, was later included in the *Fabrica* etc. (1543). Although critical of this in others, Vesalius was not above reaching conclusions relating to human structure and function through studying the ape rather than man. Only three copies of the *Tabulæ anatomicæ sex* survive: one, bound with the *Epitome* (1543: which contains nine engraved woodcuts with two others intended for that publication but eventually only included, folded, in the *Fabrica* etc.), in the library of San Marco at Venice; one bought by (Sir) William Stirling-Maxwell for 60 thalers from the Kunstkatalog of Rudolph Weigel (1804–67) of Leipzig in 1857, and donated by Stirling-Maxwell's son to the Hunterian Museum in Glasgow on 25 May 1929; and a third said to have been found by Willy Wiegand (1884–1961) in Prague in the 1940s. Three additional loose leaves were once known: two are now lost, one of which Stirling-Maxwell could have bought for another 60 thalers had he been so motivated. Stirling-Maxwell's 1874 reprint is in an edition of thirty copies.

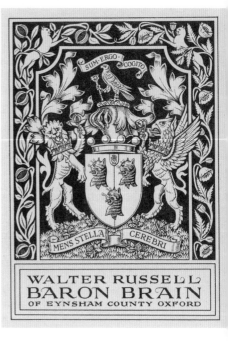

ABOVE: Bookplates of Richard Hale (1670–1728), George Edwards (1694–1773), David Lloyd Roberts (1835–1920) and Russell Brain (1895–1966)

TWENTIETH CENTURY

HORACE MALLINSON BARLOW
(1884–1954). [Bookplates].

A collection of bookplates mounted on cards in alphabetical order comprising 600 from the eighteenth century, 900 from the nineteenth and twentieth centuries and 800 others, excluding more than 500 pasted into individual books.

Together, several boxes. [MS2324, 2325, 2326-2230, 2331, 2332, 2333, 2334, 2335].

[*With*] **Horace Barlow. [Desiderata] No date.**

Typescript of desiderata containing names in alphabetical order with brief description of the design of the plate and with items acquired scored through.

Folio, 37 leaves, paginated as 74. 330 x 205 mm. In a plain card folder. [MS2336].

Inscribed: HM Barlow working copy.

Annotations: correcting entries or specifying particular details.

Horace Barlow (assistant librarian 1907–23; secretary 1923–1944) systematically collected bookplates over many years. The collection was donated by Barlow on 27 June 1952. Bookplates were introduced in Germany. The Hans Igler plate (n.d: 1450) depicts a hedgehog (the text reading 'Hans Igler that the hedgehog may kiss you'); and that of Hildebrande Brandenburg (n.d: c.1470) shows a shield of arms supported by an angel. Early English examples are from the sixteenth century: those of (Sir) Nicholas Bacon (1510–79: produced in 1574 to record books given to the University of Cambridge), (Sir) Thomas Tresham (1543–1605) and Joseph Holand (n.d.). The earliest medical bookplate is that of John Collins (c.1576–1634), Regius Professor of physic in Cambridge. Designs in the seventeenth century typically consisted of an armorial shield surrounded by an ornamental frame resembling carved oak resting on a bracket that contained the owner's name and, perhaps, a Latin motto. Later the armorial design was rejected in favour of landscape and much more personal features, or styles reflecting the artistic fashions of the period. Bookplates became more popular in the eighteenth century, when books were still expensive by comparison with income, although the engraved plate was not cheap (around two guineas). Most were specially designed; others were generic, leaving space for the owner's name to be written in manuscript. The ability to remove and replace bookplates led to some trade in 'improving' ownership, thereby adding value to individual books in commercial circulation.

JOSEPH FRANK PAYNE (1840–1910).
[Catalogue].

Catalogue of the valuable and extensive collection of early medical works (including anatomy and surgery) also a large and important collection of books & tracts on pestilence from the earliest times to the eighteenth century. The property of John Frank Payne MD FRCP (deceased), Hon. Fellow of Magdalen College, Oxford; Emeritus Harveian Professor Librarian to the Royal College of Physicians; consulting physician to St Thomas' Hospital; late President of the Pathological, Epidemiological and Dermitological Societies. Which will be sold by auction by Messrs Sotheby, Wilkinson & Hodge ... on Wednesday, 12th of July, 1911, and Two following Days, at one o'clock precisely.

London, Sotheby, Wilkinson and Hodge. 1911.

Octavo, 49 leaves, paginated as [2] 96. 245 x 155 mm. Contemporary binder's cloth.

Annotations: (1) correction of errors (Joseph for John, Professor removed, and Dermatological for Dermitological); (2) the whole collection [lots 1–731] sold for £2300.

[Bound with] Joseph Frank Payne. Catalogue of the remaining portion of the library of the late Joseph Frank Payne ... comprising his collection of rare herbals and other natural history books, a series of the first and later editions of John Milton's writings and Miltoniana, and old and modern books in general literature which will be sold at auction ... on Tuesday, the 30th of January, 1912 and following Day at one o'clock precisely.

London, Sotheby, Wilkinson and Hodge. 1912.

Octavo, 33 leaves, paginated as [2] 64.

Inserted: (1) contemporary newspaper clipping indicating that this collection failed to sell as one lot but the individual items fetched about £800; (2) and (3) clippings reporting on the sale. [22024].

Annotated: (1) extensively with prices realised for lots 1–116: £791 9s 6d; lots 236–474: 2nd portion (i.e. lots 1–474) £2053 17s 0d, Total £4353 17s 0d; (2) a note that the first day's sale realised £1089.

[Bound with] Joseph Frank Payne. The property of the late Dr Joseph Frank Payne (returned from the sale of his Library, being imperfect, and now sold not subject to return).

London, Sotheby, Wilkinson and Hodge. 1912.

Octavo, 3 leaves, paginated as 41–46.

Annotated: May 16 + 17, 1912.

The collection of early medical works sold on the first day as a single lot for £2300 to (Sir) Henry Wellcome (1853–1936). Secretive, and patient as a panther in acquiring items, Wellcome was assisted, among others, by C. J. S. Thompson (1862–1943), who used as alias the fictitious firm of Epworth and Co., Newman Street. This was an empty room. Purchases were picked up from sales in an unmarked van. Newspaper clippings pasted into the Payne sale catalogue carry the warning: 'A nightmare awaits the literary hypochondriac. In his leisure the late John (sic) Payne collected a mass of early medical literature on plague, pestilence, and famine, and the cognate ills of the flesh.' The correspondent then lists items that caught his eye and concludes: 'Altogether there is much for a liverish layman to read on a dull day.' Another clipping, after the auction, describes the sale of Milton's Of education: to Master Samuel Hartlibb (1644) for £172 to Quaritch, who bought other Miltoniana including a copy of Paradise lost (1744) for £44.0s.0d. The first issue of the first three books of Spenser's The faerie queene made £43.0s.0d. A copy of Fuchs' Herbal bought by the library at Kew Gardens realised £27.5s; Gerard's Herbal etc., (1597) made £16.10s.0d; and Herbarius patavie (1485) realised £69.0s.0d. The earliest printed book with figures of plants (Herbarium apulei platonici etc., 1488) went for £96; but evidently this was returned and re-offered in May 1912 because of 'the slightly defective title-page and the fourth page made imperfect by the figures being erased, etc.'

CATALOGUE

OF

THE REMAINING PORTION OF

THE LIBRARY

OF THE LATE

JOSEPH FRANK PAYNE, M.D. F.R.C.P.

Librarian to the Royal College of Physicians; Hon. Fellow of Magdalen College, Oxford; Emeritus Harveian Professor; Consulting Physician to St. Thomas's Hospital; late President of the Pathological, Epidemiological and Dermatological Societies,

COMPRISING HIS

COLLECTION OF RARE HERBALS AND OTHER
NATURAL HISTORY BOOKS,

A SERIES OF THE FIRST AND LATER EDITIONS OF
JOHN MILTON'S WRITINGS AND MILTONIANA,

AND

Old and Modern Books in General Literature.

WHICH WILL BE SOLD BY AUCTION,

BY MESSRS.

SOTHEBY, WILKINSON & HODGE,

Auctioneers of Literary Property & Works illustrative of the Fine Arts,

AT THEIR HOUSE, No. 13, WELLINGTON STREET, STRAND, W.C.

On TUESDAY, the 30th of JANUARY, 1912, and following Day,

AT ONE O'CLOCK PRECISELY.

May be Viewed Two Days prior.   Catalogues may be had.

DRYDEN PRESS: J. DAVY & SONS, 8-9, FRITH-STREET, SOHO-SQUARE, W.

'A nightmare awaits the literary hypochondriac. In his leisure . . . Payne collected a mass of early medical literature on plague, pestilence, and famine, and the cognate ills of the flesh . . . there is much for a liverish layman to read on a dull day.'

LEFT AND BELOW: The sale of Joseph Payne's library (part 2, 1912) with aggregate sales from the first and second portions

folio. Amsterdam, 1698

2 - 0   473   Works (Poetical), containing Paradise Lost, Paradise Regain'd, Samson Agonistes, and his Poems on Several Occasions; together with Explanatory Notes on each Book of the Paradise Lost, and a Table never before Printed, *fine portrait by R. White, and full-page engravings by M. Burghers, old calf (morocco back), old ex-libris of R. Dashwood on back of title* *folio. Printed for Jacob Tonson,* 1695

2 - 0 - 0   474   Ziegler (Casp.) Circa Regicidium Anglorum Exercitationes; acced. Jac. Schelleri Dissertatio ad Loca quaedam Miltoni, *Lugd. Bat. Sambax.* 1653 — Alex. Mori Fides Publica contra Calumnias Jo. Miltoni, *Hag. Com. A. Vlacq,* 1654; in 1 vol. *old calf, with Lamoignon arms*   *sm. 8vo*

END OF SALE.

Dryden Press: J. Davy & Sons, 8-9, Frith-street, Soho-square, W.

Total. First Portion sold July 1911.   £ 2300 - 0 - 0

2nd Portion . .   £ 2053 - 17 - 0

Total   £ 4353. 17. 0.

ARCHIBALD GARROD (1857–1936).
Inborn errors of metabolism.

INBORN ERRORS OF
METABOLISM

The Croonian Lectures delivered before
the Royal College of Physicians
of London, in June, 1908

By
ARCHIBALD E. GARROD
D.M., M.A. OXON.
Fellow of the Royal College of Physicians.
Assistant Physician to, and Lecturer on Chemical Pathology
at St. Bartholomew's Hospital.
Physician to the Hospital for Sick Children,
Great Ormond Street

" Ἐν οἴδας πολὺ χρειωδεστέρου ἔχοντι τι δοκιμασεῖν."
Aristotle, Περὶ ζῴων μορίων, I. 5.

LONDON
HENRY FROWDE   HODDER & STOUGHTON
OXFORD UNIVERSITY PRESS   20, WARWICK SQUARE, E.C.
1909

TOP: William Croone (1633–84)

Inborn errors of metabolism. The Croonian lectures
delivered before the Royal College of Physicians of
London, in June 1908.

London, Henry Frowde, Oxford University Press and
Hodder and Stoughton. 1909.

Octavo, 88 leaves, paginated as viii, 168. 190 x 125 mm. Original
cloth. [21398].

Inscribed: H.D.R [Rolleston] from A.E.G [Garrod].

Archibald Garrod coined the term 'inborn error of
metabolism'. This built upon nineteenth-century
accounts recognising that some individuals are
more and others less liable to develop a particular
condition, and that disease may be handed down
from parents to child. When (Charles-Joseph)
Bouchard (1837–1915) proposed an underlying
chemical basis for predisposition to gout, Garrod
pointed out that the relevance of uric acid had been
suggested by his father, (Sir) Alfred Baring Garrod
(1819–1907). Emil Fischer (1838–1914: Nobel
Prize for Chemistry 1902) showed that proteins
are degraded not as a whole but as individual
amino acids by specialised enzymes; and Reginald
(John) Ryle (1853–1922) defined diathesis as 'a
transmissible variation in the structure or function
of tissue[s] rendering them peculiarly liable to
react in a certain way to certain extrinsic stimuli'.
Garrod elucidated the autosomal recessive pattern
of inheritance and postulated that inborn errors
of metabolism result from mutation in both copies
of a single gene encoding one enzyme. Here, he
summarises his studies on alkaptonia, cystinuria,
pentosuria and albinism. William Croone (1633–84)
wrote *De ratione motus musculorum* (1664: a rare
treatise which the College has bound-up with other
tracts). Croone bequeathed his medical books to the
College of Physicians, the Croonian lecture being
founded by his widow in Croone's memory. This is
often confused with the Croonian lecture of the
Royal Society also established in his name.

JOSEPH FRANK PAYNE (1840–1910).
[History of the College Club].

History of the College Club of the Royal College of Physicians of London. By Joseph Frank Payne, MD. Fellow and Harveian Librarian to the College. Sit perpetua.

London, Privately printed. 1909.

Quarto, 90 leaves. paginated as x [2] 112 lvi. Engraved frontispiece (by Emery Walker Ph.sc. of Sir Lucas Pepys Bart, member of the College Club, 1774–1830). 215 x 170 mm. Contemporary morocco with blind and gilt-tooling of the College coat of Arms (by Sangorski & Sutcliffe, London). [34521].

Annotated: This history of their society, which has been received with the greatest satisfaction by all the members of the College Club, is now presented to their most learned colleague Dr Joseph Frank Payne, its author, by the present members of the Club whose signatures are on the opposite page and who at a meeting of the Club held on Monday February 28: 1910 unanimously voted their thanks to him and expressed their admiration for his work; (2) [Signatures of] R. Douglas Powell, W. S. Church, Dyce Duckworth, Edwd Liveing, P. W. Latham, Thomas Barlow, W. H. Allchin, Frederick Taylor, Ge H Savage, Thomas Buzzard, T. Henry Green, Norman Moore, Seymour J. Sharkey, Wm Osler, Wm Cayley, J. A. Ormerod, F. H. Champneys, James Reid; (3) markings against selected members' names in the text (presumed to be those active in 1909).

[With] Arthur MacNalty. History of the College Club of the Royal College of Physicians of London. Volume 2 1926–1961. By Sir Arthur Salusbury MacNalty KCB MD Fellow of the College. Sit perpetua.

London, privately printed. 1964.

Quarto, 88 leaves. paginated as [4] 7 [1] 8 (sic)–167 [4]. 222 x 175 mm. Original stiff paper wrappers. [50305].

Stamped: Wills Library Guy's Hospital Medical School SE1 9RT.

Inscribed: Don't stick labels over these signatures, CP Symonds, Dick Bomford, Geoffrey Marshall, Anthony Feiling, Arthur Salusbury MacNalty, Harold Himsworth, Adrian, JJ Conybeare, TF Fox, Henry H Dale, G Marshall, Brain, FJ Nattrass, AH Cooke, Thomas Hunt.

The College Club, formed in 1764, aspired to be 'an assembly of good fellows meeting under certain conditions', by which was meant a tavern. It adopted the motto Sit perpetua (It should be uninterrupted). An older College Club existed but the two merged in 1805 and the College Social Club joined in 1820. Members were required to be fellows of the College, graduates of the Universities of Oxford or Cambridge, and 'clubbable'. Payne lists 155 past and present physicians who were members together with their domestic addresses; and MacNalty extends this to 231. The first was Anthony Askew and the last Max (Lord) Rosenheim. The Club first met at St Alban's tavern, the Star and Garter in Bond Street and then the Thatched House tavern in St James' Street, before moving to the Burlington, Bristol and Continental Hotels. The dinners were not spartan affairs; the cost for seven members on 25 January 1774 was £5.13s.6d, increasing to £1 per head by 1815. Honours, promotion and marriage occasioned a gift of wine or turtle to the Club, as did losing one of the bets placed by members on matters of opinion, politics or future events on which the rest of the Club adjudicated. Membership was generally for life: (Sir) Lucas Pepys (1742–1830) dined with the Club continuously for fifty-five years. Photographs of members were collected from 1865 and, from 1874, each person present signed his (and later her) name in a book. In the twentieth century, meetings continued at the Burlington and subsequently, the Langham Hotel, until this was bombed in the Second World War, and thereafter mainly at the Trocadero. Meetings outside London were introduced from 1953. Dinners with guests who were not fellows of the College were instituted in 1959, and at about that time a reciprocal annual dinner with the Royal Society dining club, dating from c. 1650, was started. Over the years the Club collected various items of silver, an inkstand and a cricket ball used in a Somerset *vs* Glamorgan match when Frederic Poynton (1869–1943) captained the Somerset side. These are present at all meetings of the Club, which still meets quarterly at the College for dinner at 7 p.m., in evening dress, and for lunch annually in Oxford or Cambridge.

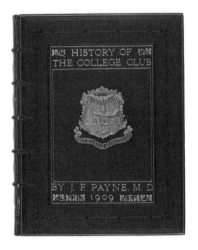

ABOVE: Dedication to Joseph Payne from members of the College Club (1909); and signed copy of the second volume (1964)

HENRY HEAD (1861–1940).
Destroyers and other verses.

Destroyers and other verses.

London, Humphrey Milford, Oxford University Press. 1919.

Octavo, 44 leaves, paginated as 86 [2]. 180 x 105 mm. Original quarter cloth with paper boards. [12225].

Inscribed: to the Library of the Royal College of Physicians by the Author Henry Head 1919.

> And valorous trophies crumbled into dust,
> Perchance my gift may glow,
> Still radiating sacrificial joy
> Amid the ravages of moth and dust.

TOP: Sir Henry (1861–1940) and Ruth Head (1866–1939)

ABOVE: *Destroyers and other verses* (1919): From 1914–1918 'I cannot stand and wait'; lines 22–25

Published in an edition of 500 copies, *Destroyers* contains poems that previously appeared in *The Yale Review*, *The English Review* and *The Dublin Review*. It is dedicated to Ruth Mayhew Head: 'To her, without whose touch the strings would have been mute.' The sections are: 1914–18 and a reprinting of *Songs of La Mouche* (1910) but omitting 'A pastoral' and 'Autumn love'. Not present in the 1910 volume but included in 1919 is the dedication of *Spring death* 'to JW who died on Active Service, 1901'. Head's later verse was much influenced by his experience with officers admitted to the Empire Hospital. The final line of the poem from which the volume takes its title reads: 'Amid the ravages of moth and dust.' Evidently, Head had misgivings about reusing 'dust', which appears four lines earlier, in the last line. Several copies of *Destroyers* (but not this one) have the final 'dust' corrected to 'rust' in Head's hand. The copy owned by Harvey Cushing (1869–1939) contains a note: 'H.H. told me August 1930 this should be "rust" not "dust".' A manuscript copy of the poem sent by Head to Cushing ends 'amid the ravages of moth and rust'. Another copy of *Destroyers*, dedicated by Head on 11 November 1926 'To Helen G-B', makes the same correction in his hand. However, a letter dated 8 October 1925 from Head to Sherrington, on another matter, includes a typescript dated January 1915, indicating that the poem was written for Sherrington, has 'dust' not 'rust' in the last line. The bibliography of Head (1961) describes *Songs of La Mouche and other verses* as published under the pseudonym Lucas Beck – the hero of Ruth's novel *A history of departed things* (1918) based loosely on Henry. Nothing by Beck, or the volume entitled *Pastoral* (also in the bibliography) appear to exist. Since both *Spring death* and [A] *Pastoral* appear in *Songs of La Mouche and other verses*, it seems likely that all Head's published poems appear in two volumes only, *Songs of La Mouche* (1910) and *Destroyers* (1919).

[ERIC GILL] (1882–1940).
[New Testament].

The four gospels of the Lord Jesus Christ according to the authorized version of King James I with decorations by Eric Gill … [Printed by Robert and Moira Gibbings at the Golden Cockerel Press at Waltham Saint Lawrence in Berkshire. Begun on 20th February 1931 and completed on 28th October in the same year. Compositors: F Young and AH Gibbs. Pressman: AC Cooper. Number 251 of 500 copies of which 1–12 are on vellum].

Waltham Saint Lawrence, Golden Cockerel Press. 1931.

Folio, 137 leaves, paginated as [2] 268 [4], black and white wood engraved decorations, initials, first words, and borders (text not justified). 330 x 235 mm. Original half-pigskin with cloth boards. [49279].

Stamped: bound by S&S [Sangorski and Sutcliffe] London.

Private presses sought to re-establish the aesthetic qualities of typography and book production considered to have been adversely affected by mechanisation.

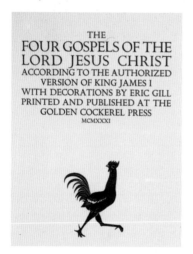

Reverend (Charles Henry Olive) Daniel (1836–1919) developed a private press at Worcester College, Oxford, with typeface based on the recently rediscovered Bishop Fell (1625–86) characters used in the foundry attached to Oxford University Press from 1675. William Morris (1834–96) turned to printing when he deemed that none of the books in which he had written were worthy of inclusion in the 1889 Arts and Crafts Exhibition. Edward Prince (1846–1923) cut Morris' first steel punches using the method of Claude Garamond. Thomas (James) Cobden-Sanderson (1840–1922) bound many of Morris' books – as did his pupil Douglas Cockerell (1870–1945). Cockerell argued that 'paper-makers, ink-makers, printers, bookbinders, and a host of other contributory craftsmen, including the author, must each do their part for a book to be harmonious'. Challenged by a client who baulked at the price of £6 for a binding with very little gold tooling, Cobden-Sanderson remarked: 'Madam, I charge as much for my restraint as for my elaboration.' He developed the Doves Press (1900–17) which recreated the Jenson Venetian typeface in its most famous book, *The English Bible* (1902), characterised by wide spacing between letters and some other idiosyncrasies. Eventually Cobden-Sanderson threw his type into the River Thames. Harold 'Hal' Midgley Taylor (1893–1925) started the Golden Cockerel Press (1920–61) for which Eric Gill (1882–1940) – a louche figure, but considered the greatest English letter cutter and a master in the art of sculpture and wood-engraving of the twentieth century – designed the Roman type used in *The four gospels*. Most of the books were bound by Sangorski and Sutcliffe at their premises in Soho.

ROBERT PLATT (1900–78), AUBREY LEWIS, J. G. SCADDING, R. BODLEY SCOTT, F. AVERY JONES, N. C. OSWALD, C. M. FLETCHER, J. N. MORRIS AND J. A. SCOTT
(twentieth century). [Smoking and health].

Smoking and health. Summary of a report of the Royal College of Physicians of London on smoking in relation to cancer of the lung and other diseases.
Pitman Medical Publishing Co. Ltd., London. 1962.

Octavo 40 leaves, paginated as S8 [2] 70. 210 x 140 mm. Original stiff paper. [35930].

In a culture where smoking was condoned and a source of much revenue for companies and the Inland Revenue, *Smoking and health* led to the habit being described as 'slow-motion suicide'. Platt responded to the suggestion of (Sir) Francis Avery Jones (1910–98), whose initiative had been rebuffed by the former President, (Russell) Lord Brain, despite the evidence for an association between smoking and lung cancer provided by Austin Bradford Hill (1897–1991) and (Sir) Richard Doll (1912–2005); and by Charles Fletcher (1911–95). Asked to get the College involved, Platt answered simply: 'Of course, we should.' But, given fiscal consequences and lobbying, this courageous and emphatic response heralded a long campaign that, in

challenging the national addiction to smoking, was bounced around the Ministry of Health and the Cabinet. At a time when 75 per cent of men, 50 per cent of women and many schoolchildren smoked cigarettes, the College report described premature death as a direct consequence of smoking. Further reports followed in 1971, 1977, 1983 and 2000 that extended the list of associated diseases and incriminated pipe and cigar smoking. These reports maintained the pressure for action and the College can take credit for having pressurised the Government and altered policy towards the present situation of a complete ban on smoking in public buildings and many open spaces.

ABOVE: High-impact front cover of *Smoking and health* (1962)

DOUGLAS BLACK (1913–2002).
[Harveian oration].

The Harveian Oration. Cui bono?
Delivered before the Fellows of
the Royal College of Physicians of
London on Tuesday 18th October
1977.

London, Royal College of
Physicians. 1977.

Octavo, 9 leaves, paginated as 18.
210 x 150 mm. Original binders red
cloth. [40135-6].

**The doctor must
be a wise trustee
of the sick, and
society should
understand the
need for medicine
to balance
multiple issues
and pressures
at any one time.
Black resents the
social model of
doctoring in which
populations and
prevention trump
patients and
prescriptions.**

Edward Emily (1617–57) delivered the first
Harveian Oration in 1656. (Sir) Douglas Black
gave the two hundred and ninety-second.
In writing on 'who gains?', Black makes the
distinction from 'what good is it?' as a rhetorical
statement on medicine in the second half of
the twentieth century. He argues that science
in medicine is laudable but something greater
must also be achieved. Medicine is for the
individual not the human race. What can be done
is not necessarily what should be done. Black
speaks for the patient in that person's social
context as part of the medico-centric doctrine
of medical practice. The relationship is complex
and asymmetric given expertise on one side
and a degree of dependence on the other. The
doctor must be a wise trustee of the sick, and
society should understand the need for medicine
to balance multiple issues and pressures at
any one time. Black resents the social model of
doctoring in which populations and prevention
trump patients and prescriptions. And, while
acknowledging the issues of cost and benefit
in the economics of medicine and options for
reducing waste and harnessing expenditure,
he shies away from too much intrusion of
healthcare economics on the organisation of
medical services, threatening as that does the
innovation and application of biomedical research.
His position is that: 'In claiming the status of a
profession, we acknowledge our duty to set the
interests of our patients above our own self-
interest; an altruistic ideal will lead to better
conduct than will a bald statement of self-interest.'
Perceiving himself to be writing in troubled times,
Douglas Black's Harveian Oration is the prescient
bellowing of an ancient and noble creature that
sees through a glass darkly what lies ahead.

OPPOSITE: Douglas Black (1913–2002)

BIBLIOGRAPHY

Anon. *A guide to the exhibition in the King's Library illustrating the history of printing, music-printing and bookbinding.* British Museum. 1901.

Anon. *A brief introduction to the library.* Royal College of Physicians of London. (n.d.).

Briggs, Asa. *A history of the Royal College of Physicians of London.* Oxford University Press, for the Royal College of Physicians, Volume 4. 2005.

Carter, John and Muir, Percy H. *Printing and the mind of man. The impact of print on five centuries of western civilization.* Cassell and Co. 1967.

Clark, George. *A history of the Royal College of Physicians of London.* Clarendon Press, for the Royal College of Physicians, Volumes 1 and 2. 1964, 1966.

Cooke, A. M. *A history of the Royal College of Physicians of London.* Clarendon Press, for the Royal College of Physicians, Volume 3. 1972.

Crawford, Alice (Ed.). *The meaning of the library.* Princeton University Press. 2015.

Creighton, Charles. *A history of epidemics in Britain.* Two volumes. Cambridge at the University Press. 1891-4.

Davenport, G., McDonald, W. I. and Moss-Gibbons, C. *The Royal College of Physicians and its collections. An illustrated history.* The Royal College of Physicians of London. 2001.

Eisenstein, Elizabeth L. *The printing revolution in early modern Europe.* Cambridge University Press. 1983.

Fine, Leon G. *Harvey's keepers. Harveian librarians through the ages.* Royal College of Physicians of London. 2007.

Fulton, John F. *The great medical bibliographers.* University of Pennsylvania Press. 1951.

Gaskell, Philip. *A new introduction to bibliography.* Oxford at the Clarendon Press. 1972.

Houston, Keith. *The book. A cover-to-cover exploration of the most powerful object of our time.* W. W. Norton. 2016.

Howsam, Leslie (Ed.). *The Cambridge companion to the history of the book.* Cambridge University Press. 2015.

Ker, N. R. *Medieval manuscripts in British libraries. Vol I London.* Oxford at the Clarendon Press. 1969.

Leedham-Green, E. and Webber, T.; Mandelbrote, G. and Manley, K.A.; and Black, A. and Hoare, P. (Eds.). *The Cambridge history of libraries in Britain and Ireland. Vol I, To 1640; Vol II 1640–1850; Vol III, 1850–2000.* Cambridge University Press. 2006.

McKerrow, Ronald B. *An introduction to bibliography for literary students.* Oxford at the Clarendon Press. 1927.

McMurtrie, Douglas C. *The Book.* Covici-Friede. 1937.

Middleton, Bernard. *A history of English craft bookbinding technique* (4th edition, revised). Oak Knoll Press and the British Library. 1996.

Myers, Robin and Michael Harris (Eds.) *Medicine, mortality and the book trade.* Oak Knoll Press. 1998.

Newman, C. E. 'The first library of the Royal College of Physicians'. (Fitz-Patrick Lecture, 1968) *Journal of the Royal College of Physicians of London.* 1969: 3; 299–307.

Newman, C. E. 'The history of the College library, 1879–99'. *Journal of the Royal College of Physicians of London.* 1984: 18; 66–73.

Nixon, Howard M. *Five centuries of English bookbinding.* Scolar Press. 1978.

Osler, William. *Bibliotheca Osleriana; a catalogue of books illustrating the history of medicine and science, collected, arranged and annotated by Sir William Osler, and bequeathed to McGill University.* Oxford at the Clarendon Press. 1929.

Payne, L. M. and Newman, C. E. 'The history of the College library: the Dorchester Library'. *Journal of the Royal College of Physicians of London.* 1970: 4; 234–46.

Payne, L. M. and Newman, C. E. 'The history of the College library 1688–1727'. *Journal of the Royal College of Physicians of London.* 1971: 5; 385–396.

Payne, L. M. 'The history of the College library: George Edwards, library keeper'. *Journal of the Royal College of Physicians of London.* 1973: 7; 145–53.

Payne, L. M. and Newman, C. E. 'The History of the College Library 1760–1792: in the time of George III'. *Journal of the Royal College of Physicians of London.* 1974: 8; 283–93.

Payne, L. M. and Newman C. E. 'The History of the college library: the last thirty years in Warwick Lane'. *Journal of the Royal College of Physicians of London.* 1974: 9; 87–98.

Payne, L. M. and Newman, C. E. 'Dr Munk, Harveian Librarian: the first period. 1977'. *Journal of the Royal College of Physicians of London.* 1977: 11; 281–288.

Payne, L. M. and C. E. Newman. 'The History of the [Royal] College [of Physicians of London] Library: the new library in Pall Mall'. *Journal of the Royal College of Physicians of London.* 1977: 11; 163–170.

Payne, L. M. and Newman, C. E. 'History of the College Library 9: Dr Munk as Harveian Librarian, 2 (1862–1870)'. *Journal of the Royal College of Physicians of London.* 1978: 12; 189–195.

Pormann, Peter. *The mirror of health: discovering medicine in the Golden Age of Islam.* Royal College of Physicians, London. 2013.

Royal College of Physicians of London. *Catalogue of the library.* 1912.

Singer, Charles and C. Rabin. *A prelude to modern science being a discussion of the history, sources and circumstances of the Tabulae Anatomicae sex of Vesalius.* Cambridge University Press for the Wellcome Historical Medical Museum. 1946.

Steinberg, S. H. and John Trevitt. *Five Hundred Years of Printing.* British Library and Oak Knoll Press. 1996.

Suarez, Michael F. and H. R. Woodhuysen (Eds.). *The Oxford companion to the book.* Two volumes. Oxford University Press. 2010.

Thornton, John L. *Medical books, libraries and collectors. A study of bibliography and the book trade in relation to the medical sciences.* Grafton and Co.1949.

Tritton, A. S. 'Catalogue of Oriental Manuscripts in the Library of the Royal College of Physicians'. *Journal of the Royal Asiatic Society.* 1951: 83; 182–192.

Turner, Helen. *Henry Wellcome: the man, his collection and his legacy.* Wellcome Trust and Heinemann. 1980.

IN THE BEGINNING
WAS THE WORD,
AND THE WORD WAS WITH GOD,
AND THE WORD WAS GOD. THE
SAME WAS IN THE BEGINNING WITH GOD. ALL
THINGS WERE MADE BY HIM; AND WITHOUT HIM
WAS NOT ANY THING MADE THAT WAS MADE. IN
HIM WAS LIFE; AND THE LIFE WAS THE LIGHT OF
MEN. AND THE LIGHT SHINETH IN DARKNESS;
AND THE DARKNESS COMPREHENDED IT NOT.